CONTENTS

Tunes included in VOLUME 65 are:

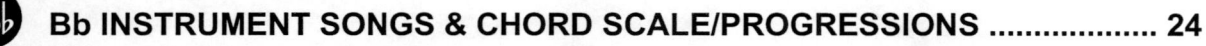 **CONCERT KEY SONGS & CHORD SCALE/PROGRESSIONS** 1

 **Bb INSTRUMENT SONGS & CHORD SCALE/PROGRESSIONS** 24

 **Eb INSTRUMENT SONGS & CHORD SCALE/PROGRESSIONS** 47

BASS CLEF INSTRUMENT SONGS & CHORD SCALE/PROGRESSIONS ... 70

> Any codas (⊕) that appear will be played only once
> on the recording at the end of the <u>last</u> recorded chorus.

PLAY-A-LONG CD INFORMATION

STEREO SEPARATION: RIGHT CHANNEL=Organ & Drums; LEFT CHANNEL=Bass & Drums
TUNING NOTES: Concert Bb & A (A=440)

PERSONNEL ON PLAY-A-LONG RECORDING

HANK MARR - Hammond B3 Organ; STEVE DAVIS - Drums
JAMEY AEBERSOLD (OVERDUB) - *Right Hand, ⁺Bass Lines

Music Engraving & Graphics
PETE GEARHART

Published by
JAMEY AEBERSOLD JAZZ®
P.O. Box 1244
New Albany, IN 47151-1244
www.jazzbooks.com
ISBN 978-1-56224-223-7

ONLINE AUDIO TRACKS
https://go.aws/3eBIG11

All CD tracks
correspond to the
online tracks

BOOK ONLY: $5.95 U.S.

INTRODUCTION

If you're just getting into tunes and want to learn basic jazz repertoire, this set is for you! Organist Hank Marr and drummer Steve Davis (Jamey Aebersold can be heard on organ here and there doing a few touch-ups) provide a solid foundation for your improvisations, and the tempos aren't too demanding. After you've mastered this set, you may want to try other Play-A-Longs with the same tunes for variety and challenge.

Most of the tunes on this set were written by jazz musicians with an eye toward creating a good vehicle for improvisation. Mile Davis is associated with several; he composed **Four** and **Tune Up** in the early fifties, though some sources claim that blues saxophonist-singer Eddie "Cleanhead" Vinson actually wrote them. Davis definitely did not write **Bye Bye Blackbird**, **Stablemates**, **But Not For Me**, and **Oleo**, but his recordings of these tunes were important in establishing them as jazz standards.

From about 1953 to 1968, one often got the impression that Davis was choosing the repertoire for many other jazz groups by what he recorded. John Coltrane, who first came to prominence in the Miles Davis Quintet, wrote **Giant Steps** and **Moment's Notice**, both of which present unique improvising challenges. Tommy Flanagan, who was the pianist on the original "Giant Steps" recording, has said that Coltrane gave him the tune to look at a week before the session, but had not indicated that it was to be played up-tempo! There is a story that when Coltrane brought an untitled original to a Blue Note record date, trombonist Curtis Fuller took look at it and said, "Do you really expect me to play this on a moment's notice?," giving Coltrane his title for that tune.

Saxophonist Benny Golson has written a number of tunes that have become jazz standards, **Along Came Betty** and **Stablemates** among them. The chromatic movement of the chord changes in both tunes and the 14-bar section length in **Stablemates** keep the soloist from getting bored, to say the least. Both tunes reveal some Golson autobiography - **Along Came Betty** commemorates a girlfriend, and **Stablemates** pays tribute to band leader-educator Herb Pomeroy who Golson was friendly with during his time in Boston in the mid-fifties. Golson used to sit in a lot with Pomeroy's group that played at the Stable, a legendary club there.

Charlie Parker's contributions to this set are **Confirmation** and **Blues For Alice**. **Confirmation** is still played a lot on sessions, and the chord structure of **Blues For Alice** (note the similarity in the harmony of the two tunes, as if **Blues For Alice** were a blues application of the ideas in **Confirmation**) as been used for countless other blues lines since.

The man Parker once introduced as "My worthy constituent," Dizzy Gillespie, wrote **Algo Bueno** (aka *Woody 'N You*) in the forties for Woody Herman, but when Woody didn't use it, Dizzy put it in his own band's book with the **Algo Bueno** ("something good") title.

Nica's Dream was written by Horace Silver in honor of the Baroness Pannonica de Koenigswarter, a descendent of the Rothschild family whose patronage of Thelonious Monk also wrote tunes for her. **Jeannine** was the pianist-producer Duke Pearson's contribution to the jazz repertoire. Sonny Rollins's **Oleo** is probably the most played variant on the "Rhythmn" changes today (older players also use *Lester Leaps In* and *Cottontail*, and Thelonious Monk's *Rhythm-A-Ning* has its adherents).

Teenage composer Billy Strayhorn approached Duke Ellington in 1938 hoping to write for the band, the piece he gave Ellington for appraisal was *Lush Life*. Ellington (who never recorded the tune) took him on as a lyricist and have Strayhorn, a Pittsburgh native, his new York apartment to work in while he and the band were on a European tour. When Ellington came back several months later, he found that Strayhorn had used the time to study Ellington's scores and (incidentally) compose **Take The "A"**

Train, a tune that's been done in every conceivable style from a waltz (Oscar Peterson) to rhythm ballad (Glenn Miller). The title refers to a Manhattan subway train (once know as the IRT) and Stayhorn's lyric gives a romantic account of it. Could this lyric have been on Bobby Troup's mind when he wrote *Route 66* a couple of years later?

Ellington's valve trombonist Juan Tizol wrote **Perdido**; later arranger Tadd Dameron wrote a bop melody on the changes called Wahoo that often is heard as an outchorus when **Perdido** is played. Speaking of Tadd Dameron, **Good Bait** was very popular among musicians in the forties and fifties. The monothematic idea of using the transposed "A" section as a release is not new; in fact, the ballad *What's New*, written several years earlier, as the same melodic economy.

Also on this set are several tunes written by professional, popular songwriters who no doubt were pleased with the interest shown in their work by jazz players, but did not write specifically for them. Ray Henderson, who is represented here by **Bye Bye Blackbird**, is best remembered for his song writing and publishing venture with BG DeSylva and Lew Brown in the twenties.

Also from the twenties is **Mean To Me**, written by a couple of vaudeville men. **Speak Low**, **September Song**, and **But Not For Me** come from Broadway shows, written (the first two by Kurt Weill, the latter by George Gershwin) by men who had also composed successful concert music. Gershwin was probably closer to the jazz world than Weill; the mutual respect that he and jazz musicians had for each other is well documented.

Karl Sussdorf, a native of Valdez, Alaska, worked as a pianist/arranger in Hollywood and New York; Benny Carter was among his collaborators. He's best known for writing **Moonlight In Vermont** with lyricist John Blackburn; guitarist Johnny Smith's version with Stan Getz in the early fifties became a juke box hit.

Bart Howard, who wrote **Fly Me To The Moon** (**In Other Words**), is a pen name for Howard Gustafson. He was cabaret legend Mabel Mercer's accompanist for four years.

Building a repertoire is an important part of becoming a good jazz musician; the story of an exasperated Sonny Stitt yelling "Don't you know any tunes?," at a young bass player (who has since played and recorded with many leading musicians) has occurred countless times on countless bandstands. Learning the tunes on this set will go a long way toward ensuring that such a humiliation won't happen to you.

CONTRAFACT LIST

Other tunes with the same chord changes as tunes on this set:

Algo Bueno	Woody 'N You, Woody 'N' I, Philly JJ, Dizzy Moods
Along Came Betty	In A Way She Goes
Confirmation	Doujie, Duck Soup, Denial, Striver's Row, I Know, Commutation, 26-2 ("Confirmation" with "Giant Steps" superposition)
Giant Steps	Koncepts, J.W., Dear John, Theme For Penny
I Got Rhythm (32-Bar Version)	Oleo, Cotton Tail, Anthropology, Moose The Mooche, Meet The Flintstones, Straighten Up and Fly Right, Wee (aka Allen's Alley), Shaw 'Nuff, Lester Leaps In, Rhythm-A-Ning, Little Pixie, Tip Toe
Perdido	Wahoo, Air Pocket
Tune Up	Countdown ("Giant Steps" superposition)

Vol. 65 DISCOGRAPHY

NOTE: Unless marked LP or Cassette, the listed album numbers are for CD issues. If an item was out of print at press time it is marked "OP." "BB" = Big Band. Items within parentheses are different issues of the same take. (Probable first recording is marked "*").

Algo Bueno (aka Woody'n You)
Music By Dizzy Gillespie. Introduced by Dizzy Gillespie Big Band.

As Algo Bueno:
Roy Eldridge/Dizzy Gillespie (Verve 314 521 647-2)
Dizzy Gillespie Big Band (RCA Bluebird 66528-2)(Vogue 09026-68213-2)
Charlie Parker (PHG W-843-2)
As Woody'n You:
Conte Candoli w. Christlieb (Best Recordings BR-92101-2)
John Coltrane (Prestige 16PCD-4405-2)
Curtis Counce (Contemporary OJCCD-7655-2; OJCCD-159-2)
Miles Davis (Blue Note B2 81501)(Fresh Sound FSR CD-124)(Prestige OJCCD-190-2; PCD-012-2)
Eric Dolphy (Prestige OJCCD-416-2)
Bill Evans (Riverside RCD-018-2)
Clare Fischer & Latin Jazz Sextet (Trend TRCD-551)
Tommy Flanagan (Pablo PACD-2405-410-2; OJCCD-372-2)
Red Garland (Prestige OJCCD-481-2)
Stan Getz (Natasha NI-4005)
Dizzy Gillespie w. Mitchell-Ruff Duo (Mainstream JK 57149; 57389)
Dizzy Gillespie (Pilz America 445401; 445404-2)
Johnny Griffin (Riverside OJCCD-1827-2)
Lin Halliday (Delmark DE-449)
Barry Harris (Riverside OJCCD-208-2)
Hampton Hawes (Contemporary OJCCD-639-2)
Coleman Hawkins (Delmark DD-459)
Woody Herman BB (S. Hampton arr.)(Concord CCD-4170; CCD-4557)
Milt Jackson (Rhino 7 90991-2)
Ahmad Jamal (MCA-Chess CHD-9108)(Pair PCD-2-1244)
Keith Jarrett/Gary Peacock/Jack DeJohnette (ECM 21440-2)
Steve Marcus (Red Baron JK 53751)
Modern Jazz Quartet (Atlantic 1231-2)(Pablo PACD-2308-244-2)
Carl Perkins (Fresh Sound FSR-CD 10)
Oscar Peterson (Verve 823 470-2; 314 516 320-2; 314 519 853-2)
Bud Powell (Discovery 71007-2)(Roulette B2-93902; 30083)
Bud Powell (Verve 314 521 669-2)
Seldon Powell (Fresh Sound FSR-CD93)
Sonny Rollins (Blue Note B2-46517-2)
Gonzalo Rubalcaba (Blue Note B2-30490)
Rumsey's Lighthouse All-Stars (Contemporary CCD-14051-2)
David Sanchez (Columbia CK 57848)
Three Sounds (Gene Harris)(Blue Note B2-27323)

Along Came Betty (1957)
Music by Benny Golson. Lyrics later added by Jon Hendricks.

Art Blakey (Blue Note B2-46516*)
Art Farmer/Benny Golson Jazztet (Contemporary CCD-14034-2)(Soul Note SN-1066CD)
Curtis Fuller (Savoy CY-75624)
Benny Golson (Dreyfus 191057)
Quincy Jones (A&M 75021-3191-2)
Dave Mackay Trio (MAMA Foundation 1APDM31J-1)
Shelly Manne (Trend TRCD-527)
Pat Martino (Muse MCD-5039)
Mark Murphy (Muse MCD-5355)
Tito Puente (Concord CCD-4448)
Jimmy Raney (Criss Cross CRISS 1009 CD)
Rufus Reid Trio w. Jim McNeely (Sunnyside SSC 1010D)
John Swana Quintet (Criss Cross CRISS 1045 CD)
Phil Woods Quartet (Clean Cuts CCD 702)

Blues for Alice (1951)
Music by Charlie Parker.

Tony Furtado (Rounder CD-0277)
Major Holley (Timeless CD SJP 364)
Roland Kirk (Mercury 826 455-2; Mercury 846 630-2)
Charlie Parker (Verve 849 393-2; 833 288-2; 837 141-2*)
Red Rodney (Steeplechase SCCD 31238)
Archie Shepp/Niels-Henning Oersted Pedersen Duo (Steeplechase SCCD 31149)
Mark Whitfield (Verve 314 523 591-2)

But Not For Me (1930)
Music by George Gershwin, words by Ira Gershwin. Introduced by Ginger Rogers in the musical "Girl Crazy." Influential jazz recordings by Miles Davis (Prestige) and Ahmad Jamal (MCA-Chess).

Johnny Adams (Rounder CD-2125)
Monty Alexander/Ray Brown/Herb Ellis (Concord CCD-4193)
Gene Ammons (Prestige OJCCD-395-2)
Gene Ammons/Sonny Stitt (Prestige OJCCD-708-2)
Gene Ammons/Sonny Stitt/Jack McDuff (Ammons feat.)(Prestige PCD-24118_2)
Chet Baker (Blue Note B2-92932; Mosaic MD3-122)(Enja R2-79626)(Stash ST-CD-584)(Steeplechase SCCD 31122)
Gary Bartz (Atlantic 82720-2)
Bernard Berkhout's Swingmates (Timeless CD SJP 360)

Ran Blake (Hat Hut CD 6077)
Ruby Braff/George Barnes Quartet (Concord CCD-6005)
Teresa Brewer (Red Baron AK 48850)
Barbara Carroll (DRG 91407)
Rosemary Clooney (Concord CCD-4112)
John Coltrane (Rhino R2-1361)
Harry Connick Jr. (Columbia CK 45319)
Eddie Lockjaw Davis/Shirley Scott (Prestige OJCCD-218-2)
Miles Davis (2 takes)(Prestige OJCCD-245-2; 8PCD-012-2)
Joey DeFrancesco (Columbia CK 45443; CK 46875)
Bill Evans (solo piano - length 1:21)(Fantasy 9FCD-1012-2)
Ella Fitzgerald w. Ellis Larkins (Decca GRD-636)
Ella Fitzgerald w. Nelson Riddle (Verve 825 024-2)
Ella Fitzgerald/Andre Previn (Pablo PACD-2312-140-2)
Red Garland (Galaxy OJCCD-472-2)(Prestige OJCCD-073-2)
Red Garland/Ron Carter/Philly Joe Jones (Galaxy OJCCD-472-2)
Dexter Gordon (Black Lion BLCD-760133)
Stan Getz (Bandstand BDCD 1533)
Stephane Grappelli (Black Lion 760139)(Concord CCD-4169)
Great Jazz Trio (Hank Jones et al)(Denon DC-8567)
Bennie Green (trombone)(Prestige OJCCD-1752-2)
Roy Hargrove/Antonio Hart (RCA Novus 63164-2)
John Hicks (Red Baron AK 52761)
Red Holloway (Concord CCD-4322)
Ahmad Jamal (Atlantic 81258-2)(MCA-Chess CHD-9108)(Vogue 600049)(Pair PCD-2-1244)
JJ Johnson (Concord CCD-4523)
Etta Jones (Prestige OJCCD-702-2)
Thad Jones Quartet (Steeplechase SCCD 31197)
Thad Jones/Mel Lewis Quartet (A&M CD 0830)
Nancy Kelly (Amherst AMH 93317)
Peter Leitch/Ray Drummond (Reservoir RSR CD 118)
Dave McKenna (Concord CCD-4097)
Bob Mintzer (DMP CD-479)
Modern Jazz Quartet (Prestige OJCCD-057)
Paul Motian Trio (JMT 834 440-2)
Oscar Peterson (vocal/piano)(Verve POCJ-1911 IMS)
Andre Previn/Mundell Lowe/Ray Brown (Telarc CD-83309)
Ike Quebec (Blue Note B2-99427)
Claudio Roditi (Candid CD79515)
Sonny Rollins (Prestige 7PCD-4407-2)
Mary Stallings (Concord CCD-4620)
Sun Ra (Evidence ECD 22011-2)
Toni Tennille (USA USACD-596)
Sarah Vaughan (Emarcy 846 896-2; Mercury 826 327-2; Verve 314 512 379-2)
Dinah Washington (Verve 314 513 928-2)
Ben Webster/Bill Coleman (Black Lion BLCD-760141)

Bye Bye Blackbird (1926)
Music by Ray Henderson, words by Mort Dixon. Popularized by Eddie Cantor and the Duncan Sisters. Influential jazz recording by Miles Davis in 1956 (Columbia).

Ray Brown (Capri #74034-2)
Ray Brown Trio w. Ralph Moore (Concord CCD-4477)
John Coltrane (Pablo PACD-2405-417-2; OJCCD-681-2)
Eddie Lockjaw Davis Quintet (Steeplechase SCCD-31058)
Miles Davis(Columbia CK40610;CK40798;CK44151;C4K45000)(Columbia CK44257)(Columbia CK44052)(Yadeon 502)
Joey DeFrancesco (Columbia CK 48624)
Kenny Dorham (Steeplechase SCCD 36010)
Roy Eldridge (Pablo OJCCD-373-2)
Maynard Ferguson (Mosaic MD10-156)
Rachelle Ferrell (Blue Note B2-96583)
Kenny Garrett (Warner Bros. 45017-2)
Lance Hayward (Town Crier TCD 517)
Bill Henderson (Vee Jay NVJ2-909)
Fred Hersch Trio (Chesky JD90)
Terumasa Hino (Blue Note B2-81191)
Mark Isham/Prudence Johnson (Milan 35631-2)
Keith Jarrett/Gary Peacock/Jack DeJohnette (ECM 314 513 074-2)
Keith Jarrett w. Peacock, Motian (ECM 78118-21531-2)
Etta Jones (Prestige OJCCD-298-2)
Rickie Lee Jones (Geffen GEFD-24426)
Rahsaan Roland Kirk (Night/Virgin 91592-2)
Gloria Lynne (Evidence ECD 22009)
Helen Merrill (Mercury 826 340-2)
Helen Merrill/Gordon Beck (Owl JULIA 038)
Joe Morello (DMP CD-506)
Oscar Peterson (solo piano)(Verve/MPS 821 843-2; Verve 314 513 830-2)
Esther Phillips (Rhino 90670-2)
Tony Reedus (Enja 6058-2)
Bobby Short (Atlantic 81715-2; 81817-2)
Nina Simone (Roulette B2-95058)
Sonny Stitt (Evidence ECD 22088-2)
Clark Terry/Bob Brookmeyer (Mainstream MDCD 711)
Toots Thielemans (Verve 845 592-2)
20th Concord Festival All-stars (Harry Sweets Edison-Red Holloway, et al)(Concord CCD-4366)
Sarah Vaughan (Mainstream MD CDO 702)
Ben Webster/Oscar Peterson Trio (Verve 829 167-2)

Confirmation (1946)
Music by Charlie Parker.

Gene Ammons (Milestone MCD-9166-2)(Prestige OJCCD-297-2)
Art Blakey w. Brown, Silver (Blue Note B2-46520)
Katchie Cartwright (Harriton Carved Wax HCW941)
Richie Cole/Hank Crawford Quartet (Milestone MCD 9180-2)
Bob Cooper (Contemporary OJCCD-161-2)
Chick Corea (Corea not present; Michael Brecker/Steve Gadd duet)(Stretch STD-1103)
Larry Coryell (Muse MCD 5303)
Miles Davis (Fresh Sound FSCD 1000)
Lou Donaldson (Timeless CD SJP 153)
Kenny Dorham (Xanadu FDC 5164)
Bobby Enriquez (GNP Crescendo GNPD 2161)
Tommy Flanagan (Enja 4014-2)
Tommy Flanagan/Hank Jones (Galaxy OJCCD-752-2)
Mike Garson/Los Gatos (CGR CGD 1801)
Dizzy Gillespie (Spotlite LP SPJ 132*OP)(Telarc CD-83307)
Dexter Gordon (Fresh Sound FSR-CD 154)
Barry Harris/Kenny Barron Quartet (Candid CCD 79519)
Chiz Harris Quartet (Cexton CR-4321)
Chris Hunter (Paddlewheel K32Y 626)
Manhattan Jazz Quintet (Paddle Wheel 240E 6805)
Steve Marcus (Red Baron JK 53751)
Jackie McLean (Prestige OJCCD-056-2)
Modern Jazz Quartet (Atlantic 81976)
Phineas Newborn (solo piano)(L&R CDLR 45020)
Phineas Newborn Quartet (Steeplechase SCCD 36026)
Charlie Parker (Debut OJCCD-041-2X(Verve 825 671-2; 833 288-2; 314 517 173-2; 837 141-2)
Bud Powell (Verve 314 521 669-2)(Steeplechase SCCD 30007/9)
Red Rodney Quintet (Chesky JD 79)
Hilton Ruiz (Stash ST-CD-19)
George Shearing Quintet (GNP Crescendo GNPD-9055; Mosaic MD5-157)
George Shearing/Hank Jones (Concord CCD-4371)
Archie Shepp/Chet Baker (L&R LR 45006)
Archie Shepp/Niels Henning Oersted Pedersen Duo (Steeplechase SCCD 31149)
Jimmy Smith (Blue Note B2-46097)
Sonny Stitt (Atlantic SD-1418-2; Rhino R2-71256)
Supersax (Columbia CK 44436)
29th St. Saxophone Quartet (Antilles 314 510 941-2)

Fly Me To The Moon (1954)
Music and words by Bart Howard. Introduced by Felicia Sanders; best selling record by pianist Joe Harnell in 1962.

Count Basie (Reprise 9 45162-2)
Tony Bennett (Columbia CK 53153; C4K 46843)(Columbia CK 66214)
Ray Brown Trio (Concord CCD-4102)
Nat King Cole w. Shearing (Capitol C2-48332)
Astrud Gilberto (Verve 823 451-2)
Per Goldschmidt et al (Milestone MCD-9224-2)
Hampton Hawes Trio (Contemporary OJCCD-178-2)
Frank Mantooth Big Band (Sea Breeze SB-2062)
McGill Swing Band (McGill 750040-2)
Carmen McRae (Hindsight HCD-602)
Wes Montgomery (A&M CD 0822; CD 2520)
Oscar Peterson (Jazz Life 2620522)
George Shearing (Mosaic MD5-157)
Ira Sullivan (Vee Jay NVJ2-950)
Sarah Vaughan (Mercury 830 714-2)

Four (1954)
Music by Eddie Cleanhead Vinson and Miles Davis.

Ron Affif (Pablo PACD-2310-954-2)
Gene Ammons (Prestige OJCCD-129-2)
Chet Baker (Philology W-56-2)(Stash ST-CD-584)
Miles Davis (Prestige OJCCD-093-2; 8PCD-012-2; Fantasy FCD-60-015*)(Prestige OJCCD-296-2; 8PCD-012-2; DCC GZS-1063)(Columbia C2K 48821)(Yadeon 502)
Harry Sweets Edison (Riverside OJCCD-487-2)
Maynard Ferguson (Mosaic MD10-156)
Joe Henderson (Verve 314 523 657-2)
Sam Jones (Riverside OJCCD-6008-2)
Mulgrew Miller (Landmark LCD)
Phineas Newborn (Contemporary OJCCD-388-2)
Anita O'Day (Verve 837 939-2)
Sonny Rollins (Blue Note B2-46517)(RCA Bluebird 07863-66530-2)

Giant Steps (1959)
Music by John Coltrane.

Jennifer Batten (Guitar 88561-5012-2)
Mark Birmingham (Sky 7-5091-CD)
Luis Bonilla Latin Jazz All Stars (Candid CCD-79507)
John Coltrane (Atlantic SD-1311-2;SD-1541-2;Mobile Fidelity UDCD-605,Rhino R271255;R271256*)(Verve 314 521 007)
Kenny Drew Jr. (Antilles 314 514 211-2)
Paquito D'Rivera/James Moody (Candid CCD-79523)
Clare Fischer (Discovery 70934-2; 74003-2)
Hal Galper (Concord CCD-4383)
Terry Gibbs/Buddy DeFranco (Contemporary CCD-14036-2)
Stephane Grappelli/McCoy Tyner (Tyner feat.)(Who's Who in Jazz CD-21047)
Lionel Hampton (Impulse MCAD-33101)
Eddie Harris (Rhino R2 71514)
David Kikoski (Epicure EK 64441)
Lee Konitz (Musicmasters CIJD 60167M)
Mark Masters Jazz Orchestra (Capri 74031-2)

Bob Mintzer/Michael Brecker (RCA Novus 63173-2)
New York Voices (Eldridge/Nazarian lyric)(GRP GRD-9653)
Rob Parton's Jazztech Big Band (Sea Breeze CDSB-2047)
Joe Pass (Pablo PACD 2310-788-2)
Tito Puente (Concord CCD-4250)
Buddy Rich (World Wide Jazz CD-21006)
Wallace Roney (Muse MCD-5372)
Gonzalo Rubalcaba (Blue Note/Somethin' Else B2-97197)(Blue Note/Somethin' Else B2-99492)
Vanessa Rubin (Neals lyric)(RCA Novus 63127-2)
Arturo Sandoval (GRP GRD-9701)
Aki Takase (Enja 6062-2)
Toots Thielemans (Private Music 82120-2)
Sumi Tonooka (Candid CCD-79516)
McCoy Tyner (Enja ENJ-CD-6080)
Bobby Watson (Red Record 123 250-2)
World Saxophone Quartet (Black Saint 120 127-2)

Good Bait (1944)
Music by Tadd Dameron and Count Basie.

John Coltrane (DCC GZS-1046; Prestige OJCCD-021-2; 16PCD-4405-2)
Dameronia (Soul Note 121 202-2)
Miles Davis (Fresh Sound FSCD-1008)
Tommy Flanagan (Galaxy OJCCD-473-2)
Dizzy Gillespie Big Band (GNP Crescendo GNCD-23)(RCA 07863-66528-2)
Dizzy Gillespie Sextet (Columbia CK 40972*)
Steve Grossman (Dreyfuss DRY-CD-36555)
Jay Hoggard (Muse MCD 5527)
Bobby Hutcherson (Landmark LCD-1501-2)
Milt Jackson (East-West 90991-2)(Pablo PACD-2310-932-2)
Steve Kuhn Trio (Concord CCD-4554)
Shelly Manne Trio (Mobile Fidelity UDCD-JS1)
Fats Navarro w. Tadd Dameron (Milestone MCD-47041-2)
Charlie Parker w. Gillespie Big Band (Philology W-843-2)
Joe Pass (Pablo PACD-2310-951-2)
Quintetto Vocale Italiano (Soul Note 121 247-2)
Recycling (Jazzline JL 1342)
Jimmy/Stacy Rowles (Delos DE-4009)
Bob Thiele Collective (Red Baron JK 57335)
Robert Trowers (Concord CCD-4545)

Jeannine (1960)
Music by Duke Pearson, lyric by Oscar Brown, Jr.

Cannonball Adderley (Landmark LCD-1301-2*OP)
Nat Adderley (Enja ENJ-7027)
Kenny Burrell & the Jazz Guitar Band (Blue Note B2-90260)
Donald Byrd (Blue Note B2-28263)
Matt Catingub Big Band (Reference Recordings RR-14CD)
Johnny Frigo (Chesky JD119)
Gene Harris Quartet (Concord CCD-4526)
Manhattan Transfer (Atlantic 81233-2)
Ladd McIntosh (Sea Breeze CDSB-2042)
Duke Pearson (Black Lion BLCD-760149)
Melvin Rhyne (Criss Cross CRISS 1080 CD)
Mike Smith (Delmark DD-444)
Turtle Island String Quartet (Windham Hill WD-0114)
Frank Vignola (Concord CCD-4576)
Rickey Woodard (Candid CCD-79509)

Mean To Me (1929)
Music and words by Roy Turk and Fred E. Ahlert. Popularized by Ruth Etting and Helen Morgan. Sung by Doris Day in the 1955 film "Love Me or Leave Me."

Nat Adderley w. Wes Montgomery (Riverside OJCCD-363-2)
Chet Baker (Verve 838 204-2)
Ruby Braff/Buddy Tate (Black Lion BLCD-760138)
Dave Brubeck (Telard CD-83345)
Betty Carter (Impulse GRD-114)
June Christy (Hindsight HCD-219)
Rosemary Clooney (Concord CCD-4081)
Cy Coleman (DRG CDSL 5205)
Curtis Counce (Contemporary OJCCD-159-2)
Paul Desmond (CBS Associated ZK 40806)
Herb Ellis/Red Mitchell (Concord CCD-4372)
Ella Fitzgerald w. Oscar Peterson (Pablo PACD-2310-759-2)
Ella Fitzgerald w. Nelson Riddle Orch. (Verve 314 519 347)
Benny Goodman (Musicmasters 65095-2)
Coleman Hawkins (Jazz J-CD-2)
Lance Hayward (Town Crier TCD 514)
Billie Holiday (Columbia CK 44252; C3K 47724)
Helen Humes (Contemporary OJCCD-171-2)
Milt Jackson/Ray Brown (Pablo OJCCD-375-2)
Roger Kellaway/Red Mitchell (Concord CCD-4551)
Barney Kessel/Ray Brown/Shelly Manne (Contemporary OJCCD-156-2)
Lee Konitz (Black Lion BLCD-760922)
Karen Mantler (XtraWATT/5; 78118-23206-2)
Frank Mantooth (Clark Terry feat.)(Optimism OP CD-3229)
Dave McKenna (Concord CCD-4313)
Jackie McLean (New Jazz OJCCD-098-2)
Carmen McRae (Denon CY-1216)
Wes Montgomery (same master as Nat Adderley listing)(Riverside 12RCD-4408-2)
Oscar Peterson/Harry Sweets Edison Duo (Pablo OJCCD-738-2)
King Pleasure (Blue Note B2-84463)
Quintetto Vocale Italiano (Soul Note 121 247-2)
Diana Ross (Motown 37463-0758-2; 37463-6340)
Sonny Stitt (Prestige PCD-24115-2)

Art Tatum (GNP Crescendo GNPD-9025)(Pablo PACD-2405-435-2; 7PACD-4404-2)
Various Artists (Frank Rosolino feat.)(Savoy SV-0188)
Sarah Vaughan (Columbia C2K 44165)(Jass J-CD-16)(Roulette B2-94983)
Teddy Wilson (solo piano)(Chiaroscuro CD(D) 111)
Teddy Wilson w. Billie Holiday (Columbia CK 40847)
Lester Young Trio w. Nat King Cole (piano)(Verve 314 521 650-2)

Moment's Notice (1957)
Music by John Coltrane.

Kenny Burrell (Contemporary CCD-14058-2)
Al Cohn/Zoot Sims (RCA Bluebird 6469-2-RB)
John Coltrane (Blue Note B2-46095; B2-99175; Mobile Fidelity UDCD-547*)
Harry Connick, Jr. (Columbia CK 53172)
Chick Corea/Lionel Hampton (Who's Who In Jazz CD-JAZ-1)
Larry Coryell (Muse MCD-5350)
Fred Hersch Trio (Chesky JD116)
Bob James (CBS Associated ZK 45218)
Hubert Laws (Epic Associated/Legacy ZK 45479)
Hendrik Meurkens (Concord CCD-4585)
Buddy Rich (Who's Who In Jazz CD-21006)
Hilton Ruiz (RCA Novus 3123-2-N)
Pharoah Sanders (Evidence ECD-22020)
Mike Stern (Atlantic 82419-2)
McCoy Tyner (Milestone MCD-55003-2)

Moonlight In Vermont (1944)
Music by Karl Suessdorf, words by John Blackburn. Best selling record
by Margaret Whiting.

Dorothy Ashby (Prestige PCD-24120-2)
Jeanie Bryson (Telarc CD-83348)
Don Byas (BLack Lion BLCD-760167)
Nat King Cole Trio (Capitol B2 98288)
Chris Connor (Atlantic 81817-2)
Joey DeFrancesco (Columbia CK 53805)
Billy Eckstine (Roulette B2-98583)
Ella Fitzgerald/Louis Armstrong (Laserlight 15706)(Verve 825 374 2)
Ella Fitzgerald/Joe Pass (Pablo PACD-2310-921-2)
Stan Getz (Fresh Sound FSCD-1003)(Natasha N1-4005)(Roulette B2-98144)(Verve 831 368-2; 314 517 171-2)
Stephane Grappelli (Who's Who 21035)
Stephane Grappelli/Earl Hines (Black Lion BLCD-760168)
Stephane Grappelli/Stuff Smith (Pablo PACD-2310-907-2)
John Hicks (Velocity VCD-82863)
Billie Holiday (Mobile Fidelity MFCD 840)(Verve 823 449-2)
Ahmad Jamal (MCA-Chess CHD-9108)(Vogue 600049)
Wynton Kelly (Blue Note B2-84456)
Andy LaVerne (Concord CCD-4577)
Frank Mantooth (Kevin Mahogany, vcl)(Sea Breeze SB-2046)
Bud Powell (Verve 314 521 669-2)
Marcus Roberts (RCA Novus 01241-63149-2)
Johnny Smith (w. Getz)(Roulette B2-97747)
Sonny Stitt (Denon DC-8566)
Billy Taylor (Prestige OJCCD-1730-2)
Cal Tjader (Fantasy OJCCD-642-2)
Mel Torme (Decca GRD-617)
Sarah Vaughan (Mercury 826 333-2; EmArcy 824 057-2)

Nica's Dream (1956)
Music by Horace Silver.

Greg Abate (Candid CCD79530)
Joe Beck (DMP CD-444)
Art Blakey w. Silver (Columbia LP 897; Odyssey LP 32 16 0246*OP)
Kenny Burrell/Brother Jack McDuff (Prestige PRCD-24131-2)
Curtis Counce (Contemporary OJCCD-423-2)
Ronnie Cuber/Randy Brecker et al (Projazz CDJ-629)
Art Farmer Quartet w. Strings (Denon DC-8589)
Gary Foster (Concord CCD-4459)
Gene Harris/Philip Morris Superband (Concord CCD-4443)
Dave Liebman Quartet (Red Record 123 253-2)
Ellis Marsalis (solo piano)(Rounder CD-2100)
Blue Mitchell Sextet (Riverside OJCCD-765-2)
David Page/Don Scarletta Trio (Cexton CR-PI-0001)
Joe Pass (Pablo PACD-2310-946-2)
Oscar Peterson (Verve 847 203-2; 314 513 830-2)
Buddy Rich (LRC-33C38-7972)
Joe Sample (Warner Bros. 45209-2)
Archie Shepp (Denon DC-8548)
Horace Silver (Blue Note B2-84042)
Mel Torme/George Shearing Duo (Torme out)(Concord CCD-4248)
Carlos "Patato" Valdes (Messidor 15827-2)
Larry Young (New Jazz OJCCD-1831-2)

Oleo (1954)
Music by Sonny Rollins.

Alan Broadbent (solo piano)(Concord CCD-4488)
Frank Capp Trio w. Rickey Woodard (Concord CCD-4469)
Ron Carter & Friends (Milestone OJCCD-6010-2)
John Coltrane (Roulette B2-93901)
Miles Davis w. Coltrane (Prestige OJCCD-190-2; 8PCD-012-2)(Columbia/Legacy CK 47835)
Miles Davis w. Mobley (Columbia CK 44425)
Miles Davis w. Rollins (Prestige OJCCD-245-2; 8PCD-012-2*)
Eric Dolphy (Prestige OJCCD-413-2)
Bill Evans (Riverside OJCCD-068-2; 12RCD-018-2)

Maynard Ferguson (Mosaic MD10-156)
Red Garland/Ron Carter/Philly Joe Jones (Galaxy OJCCD-472-2)
Grant Green (Mosaic MD4-133)
GRP All Star Big Band (GRP GRD-9740)
Roland Hanna (solo piano)(Concord CCD-4604)(Town Crier TCD 513)
Barry Harris/Kenny Barron Quartet (Candid CCD-79519)
Donald Harrison Quintet Candid CCD-79501)
Hampton Hawes Trio (Contemporary OJCCD-455-2)
James Leary (Vital VTL-005)
Steve Marcus (Red Baron JK 53751)
Pat Martino (Prestige OJCCD-397-2)
James Morrison/Adam Makowicz Quartet (East West 91243-2)
Phineas Newborn Jr. (Contemporary OJCCD-175-2)
Joe Pass Quartet (Pablo PACD-2310-951-2)
Joe Pass/Niels Pedersen Duo (Pablo OJCCD-786-2)
Niels-Henning Oersted Pedersen/Joe Pass (live date)(Pablo PACD-2308-223-2)
Tom Peron/Bud Spangler Quartet (Monarch MR-1003)
Sonny Rollins (Prestige 7PCD-4407-2)(RCA Bluebird 2496-2-RB)
George Shearing/Mel Torme (Torme out)(Concord CCD-4219)

Perdido (1942)
Music by Juan Tizol, lyric by H.J. Langsfelder and Ervin Drake. Introduced by Duke Ellington and His Orchestra. Lyric added in1944.

Louis Armstrong (GNP Crescendo GNPD-11001)(Vanguard VCD2-91/92; VMD-73129)
Count Basie (Black Lion BLCD-760294)(Roulette 98660)
Count Basie w. Sarah Vaughan (Jass J-CD-17)
Dave Brubeck (Columbia C4K 52945)(Fantasy OJCCD-046-2)
Don Byas/Ben Webster (Verve 840 031-2)
Buck Clayton/Joe Turner (Black Lion BLCD-760170)
Vassar Clements (Flying Fish FF-70592)
Miles Davis/Jimmy Forrest (Prestige PCD-24117-2)
Roy Eldridge w. Oscar Peterson (Pablo OJCCD-373)
Roy Eldridge (Jazz Masters 75246-2)
Duke Ellington (Columbia CK40836)(Hindsight HCD-410)(Hindsight HBCD-501)(RCA/Bluebird 5659-2-RB*)(RCA 07863-66531-2)
          (SAJA91231-2)(Sony Music Special Products AGK-40012)(several other Ellington recordings are in print)
Duke Ellington/Billy Strayhorn (Oscar Pettiford feat.)(Riverside OJCCD-108-2)
Ellington All-stars (Bill Berry-Marshall Royal et al)(Drive DE2-41035)
Herb Ellis/Joe Pass (Concord CCD-6002)
Buddy Emmons/Ray Pennington (Penington out)(Step One SOR-0039)
Ella Fitzgerald (Verve 837 035-2)(Verve 314 517 818-2)
Ella Fitzgerald/JATP (same master as Charlie Parker/JATP)(Verve 314 517 898)
Full Faith & Credit BB (TBA TBCD 237)
Erroll Garner (Jazz Anthology 550042)
Stephane Grappelli/Barney Kessel (Black Lion BLCD-760158)
Lionel Hampton w. Just Jazz Allstars (GNP Crescendo GNPD-15)
Coleman Hawkins w. Cozy Cole (Decca GRD-627)
Colman Hawkins/Eldridge/Hodges (Verve 314 513 755-2)Lance Hayward (Antilles 314 510 092-2)
Woody Herman BB (Flip Philips feat.)(Concord CCD-4240; CCD-4557)
Johnny Hodges (Pablo 2PACD-2620-102-2)
Harry James BB (Columbia CK 45447; C3K 52862)
Jazz at the Philharmonic (Pablo PACD-2620-104-2)
Etta Jones (Muse MCD 5474)
Gene Krupa/Charlie Ventura et al (Clarinet Classics CCD-7006)
Cleo Laine (RCA 60960-2)
Gloria Lynne (Collectibles COL-5138)(Evidence ECD-22009)
Charles Mingus (Debut 12DCD-4402-2)
Frank Morgan (Contemporary CCD-14021)
Oliver Nelson/Jimmy Forrest/King Curtis (Prestige OJCCD-325-2)
Charlie Parker/JATP (same master as Ella Fitzgerald/JATP)(Verve 837 141-2)
Charlie Parker/Dizzy Gillespie et al (Debut OJCCD-044-2)
Oscar Peterson (solo piano)(Verve 821 843-2; 314 513 830-2)
Oscar Peterson Quartet (Pablo PACD-2310-940-2)
Oscar Peterson Jam (Pablo OJCCD-385-2)
Oscar Pettiford (Impulse GRD-143)
The Ritz (Denon CY-72526)
Red Rodney et al (Mercury 830 922-2)
Paul Smith/Monty Budwig et al (Voss D2-72937)
Art Tatum w. Hampton, Rich (Pablo PACD-2405-426-2; 7PACD-4401-2)
Cal Tjader (Fantasy FCD-24712-2)
Sarah Vaughan (Columbia C2K 44165)(Roulette B2-94983; B2-98660)(Sony Music Special Products A-660)
Charlie Watts (Continuum 19201-2)
Ben Webster (Black Lion BLCD-760125)
Joe Williams (Vanguard VMD-8508)
Phil Wilson/NDR BB (Capri 74040)

September Song (1938)
Music by Kurt Weill, words by Maxwell Anderson. Introduced by Walter
Huston in the musical "Knickerbocker Holiday." Best selling record by
Bing Crosby in 1946.

Clifford Brown w. Sarah Vaughan (Emarcy 838 306-2)(same master as Sarah Vaughan w. Brown)
Chet Baker (Riverside OJCCD-087-2)
Sidney Bechet (GNP Crescendo GNPD-9012)
Tony Bennett (Columbia/Legacy CK 46843)
Dave Brubeck Trio (Fantasy FCD-24726-2)
John Bunch (Chiaroscuro CR(D) 144)
June Christy (Hindsight HCD-235; HCD-414)
Rosemary Clooney (Concord CCD-4444)
Nat King Cole w. Shearing (Blue Note B2-99290; Capitol C2-48322)
Ella Fitzgerald (Verve 839 838-2; 843 621-2)
Erroll Garner (EmArcy 832 994-2)(Savoy SV-0244)
Dizzy Gillespie/Ray Brown/et al (Pablo OJCCD-443-2)
Gene Harris Quartet (Concord CCD-4640)
Coleman Hawkins (Savoy SV-0182)(Pablo 2PACD-2620-2)
Stan Kenton (Blue Note B2-97350)
Marian McPartland w. Rosemary Clooney (Jazz Alliance TJA-12003)
Red Norvo Trio (Savoy SV-0168)
Art Pepper (Galaxy OJCCD-475-2)

Flip Phillips (Concord CCD-4358)
John Pizzarelli (RCA Novus 02141-63182-2)
Django Reinhardt (RCA 66468-2)(Verve 835 418-2)
Betty Roche (Prestige OJCCD-1718-2)
Artie Shaw (Musicmasters 65101-2)
Art Tatum Trio (Capitol C21Y 92866)Art Tatum (solo)(Pablo PACD-2405-433-2; 7PACD-4404-2)
Art Tatum w. Hampton, Rich, et al (Pablo PACD-2405-428-2; 6PACD-4401-2)
Cal Tjader (Fantasy OJCCD-642-2)
Cal Tjader w. Mongo Santamaria (Fantasy FCD-24732-2)
Mel Torme w. Rob McConnell & Boss Brass (Concord CCD-4306)
Mel Torme (Decca GRD-617; GRP GRD-9748)
Sarah Vaughan w. Clifford Brown (Emarcy 814 641-2; 826 320-2; 314 512 379-2)
Sarah Vaughan (Mercury 826 327-2)(Musicraft MVSCD-57)

Speak Low (1943)

Music by Kurt Weill, lyric by Ogden Nash. Introduced by Mary Martin in the musical "One Touch Of Venus." Best selling record in 1944 by Guy Lombardo.

Monty Alexander (Concord CCD-4108)
Laurindo Almeida/Bud Shank (World Pacific B2-96339)
Gato Barbieri (A&M 75021-3029-2)
Gary Bartz (Candid CCD-79049)
Tony Bennett (Columbia CK 45348)
Walter Bishop Jr. (Black Lion BLCD-760109)
Nick Brignola (Reservoir RSR CD 123)
Alan Broadbent (Discovery DSCD-929)
Alan Broadbent/Gary Foster Duo (Concord CCD-4562)
John Bunch (solo piano)(Chiaroscuro CD(D) 144)
Kenny Burrell (Contemporary CCD-14065-2)
LaVerne Butler (Chesky JC91)
Charlie Byrd w. Washington Guitar Quintet (Concord CCD-42014)
Charlie Byrd/Bud Shank (Concord CCD-4173)
Frank Capp Trio w. Rickey Woodard (Concord CCD-4469)
Teddy Charles/Shorty Rogers/Jimmy Giuffre (Prestige OJCCD-1731-2)
John Coltrane w. Sonny Clark (Blue Note B2-99175)
Peter Erskine (RCA Novus 63140-2)
Booker Ervin (Candid CCD-79014)(Prestige PRCD-24123-2)
Bill Evans (Riverside OJCCD-025-2; 12RCD-018-2)(Cool & Blue C&B CD106)
Bill Evans w. Konitz, Marsh (Fantasy OJCCD-718-2; 9FCD-1012-2)
Ella Fitzgerald/Joe Pass (Pablo PACD-2310-888-2)
Grant Green (Blue Note B2-27312-2)
Charlie Hayden/Sharon Freeman (A&M 75021-5104-2)
Chiz Harris Quartet (Cexton CR-4321)
Coleman Hawkins (Prestige OJCCD-709-2)
John Hicks (solo piano)(Concord CCD-4442)
Steve Hobbs (Cexton CR-7654-D)
Billie Holiday (Verve 314 513 943-2)
Hank Jones (Concord CCD-4391)
Oliver Jones (Justin Time JUST 17-2 CD)
Barney Kessel (Contemporary OJCCD-238-2)
Harold Land (Contemporary OJCCD-162-2)
Nancy Marano & Eddie Monteiro (Denon CY-78901)
Mary Martin/Kenny Baker (MCA MCAD-10051)(little jazz interest)
Carmen McRae (Pair PCD2-1182)
Hank Mobley (Blue Note B2-81574)
Mark Morganelli & The Jazz Forum (Candid CCD-79054)
Oscar Peterson Trio (Jazz Life 2620522)
Pete Peterson & Collection Jazz Orch. (Dave Alexander feat.)(CMG CMD-8019)
Diane Schuur (GRP GRD-9713)
Woody Shaw (Muse MCD-5329)
Lonnie Liston Smith (Doctor Jazz AK 40612)
Lew Solloff (Evidence ECD-22005)(Pro Arte CDJ 656)
Cal Tjader (Concord Picante CCD-4247)(Concord CCD-4113)
Cal Tjader/Carmen McRae (Concord CCD-4189)
McCoy Tyner (MCA/Impulse MCAD-42000)
Sarah Vaughan (Mercury 826 333-2)

Stablemates (1955)

Music by Benny Golson.

Guido Basso (Innovation JCCD-0014)
Miles Davis (Prestige OJCCD-006-2; 8PCD-012-2*)
Art Farmer/Roy Haynes (Contemporary OJCCD-166-2)
Allen Farnham (Concord CCD-4521)
Stan Getz/Kenny Barron Duo (Verve 314 510 823-2)
Dizzy Gillespie (Verve 314 511-393-2)
Milt Jackson/Wes Montgomery (Riverside OJCCD-234-2; 12RCD-4408-2)
Philly Joe Jones BB (Riverside OJCCD-1792-2)
Buddy Montgomery/Eddie Harris (Landmark LCD-1512-2)
Wes Montgomery (same master as Milt Jackson/Wes Montgomery above)(Riverside 12RCD-4408-2)
Bruce Paulson (Sea Breeze SB-3017)
Mal Waldron (Prestige OJCCD-611-2)
Cedar Walton/David Williams (Red Record 123 242-2)
Mike Wofford (solo piano)(Concord CCD-4514)

Take The A Train (1941)

Music and lyric by Billy Strayhorn. Introduced by Duke Ellington and his Orchestra; used as the band's theme.

American Jazz Orchestra/John Lewis conductor (East-West 91423-2)
Ernestine Anderson (Concord CCD-4054)
Peter Appleyard (Concord CCD-4436)

George Benson (CBS Associated ZK-40298)
Norman Blake/Vassar Clements et al (Flying Fish HDS-90701)
Dollar Brand (Black Lion BLCD-760127)
Ruby Braff/Buddy Tate (Black Lion BLCD-760138)
Clifford Brown/Max Roach Quintet (EmArcy 814 646-2; 838 306-2)
Ray Brown Trio w. Gene Harris (Concord CCD-4268)
Dave Brubeck Quartet (Columbia CK 44215)(Columbia CK 45149)
Dave Brubeck w. Orchestra (Musicmasters 5051-2-C)
Ray Bryant (Pablo OJCCD-371-2)
Kenny Burrell (Fantasy FCD-79005)
Cab Calloway (Columbia CK 45336)
Capp/Pierce Juggernaut BB (Concord CCD-4040)
Clayton-Hamilton Jazz Orch. (Capri 74028-2)
Johnathan & Darlene Edwards (Corinthian 101-CD)
Teddy Edwards Quartet (Contemporary OJCCD-748-2)
Roy Eldridge/Dizzy Gillespie/Oscar Peterson (Pablo PACD-2310-816-2)
Duke Ellington BB (EmArcy 842071-2)(Hindsight HCD-410)(RCA Bluebird 5659-2-RB*)(Red Baron AK48631)(many others)
Duke Ellington/Count Basie Orchestras (Columbia CK 40586)
Duke Ellington (Oscar Peterson feat.)(Pablo PACD-2625-704-2)
Duke Ellington/Billy Strayhorn Quartet (Riverside OJCCD-108-2)
Ellington All-stars (Bill Berry-Marshall Royal et al)(Drive DE2-41035)
Buddy Emmons/Ray Pennington (SOR SOR-0039)
Ella Fitzgerald w. Duke Ellington Orch. (Verve 837 035-2; 314 519 832-2)(Verve 833 294-2)
Tommy Flanagan (Pablo OJCCD-737-2)
Laszlo Gardony (Sunnyside SSC 1062D)
Dizzy Gillespie (Verve 314 513 875-2)
Dizzy Gillespie & Mitchell-Ruff Duo (MIM JK 57149)
Dexter Gordon (Black Lion BLCD 760133)
The Great Jazz Trio (Hank Jones et al (Denon DC-8575; DC-8564)
Dave Grusin (GRP GRD-9715)
H.M.A. Salsa/Jazz Orch. (Sea Breeze CDSB-110-2)
Lionel Hampton (Musicmasters 5011-2-C)(TLR CD 83321)
Jake Hanna/Carl Fontana Band (Concord CCD-6011)
Roland Hanna (FRD FCD-741010)
Gene Harris Quartet (Concord CCD-4578)
Coleman Hawkins & Friends (Pablo PACD-2310-933-2)
Joe Henderson (Red Record RR-123 248)(Verve 314 511 779-2)
Jon Hendricks & Friends (Denon CY-76302)
Johnny Hodges (Pablo PACD-2620-102-2)
Milt Jackson (Pablo PACD-2310-944-2)(Pablo OJCCD-450-2)
Illinois Jacquet (Black Lion BLCD-760160)
Harry James (London 820 178-2)(Verve 823 229-2)
Eddie Jefferson (Riverside OJCCD-307-2)
Louis Jordan (Evidence ECD-26006)
Roger Kellaway/Red Mitchell (Concord CCD-4551)
Lincoln Center Jazz Orch. (Columbia CK 66379)
Kevin Mahogany (Enja ENJ-80722)
Bobby McFerrin (Elektra 60366-2)
Marian McPartland (Concord CCD-4326)
Don Menza Sextet (Voss D2-72931)
Glenn Miller BB (RCA 07863-66529-2)(tangential jazz interest)
Newport Jazz Festival All-stars (Concord CCD-4343)
Anita O'Day (Verve 837 939-2)
Pete Peterson & Collection Jazz Orch. (CMG CMD-8019)
Oscar Peterson (piano solo)(Verve/MPS 821 843-2)
Michel Petrucciani (piano solo)(Blue Note B2-80590)
Andre Previn Trio (Angel CDC-54917)
Quadrant (Milt Jackson et al)(Pablo OJCCD-805-2)
Dewey Redman (Evidence ECO-2207-2)
Buddy Rich (small group)(World Wide Jazz CD-21006)
Jimmy & Stacy Rowles (Delos DE-4009)
Doc Severinsen (Amherst AMH-93319)
Billy Strayhorn (Red Baron AK-52760)
Tom Talbert Orch. (Sea Breeze CDSB-2058)
Clark Terry (Red Baron JK 53750)(Riverside OJCCD-229-2)
Toots Thielemans (Denon DC-8563)
Butch Thompson/Doc Cheatham (Daring 25101-3012-2*)
Tonight Show Band/Doc Severinsen (Amherst AMH-93312)
Mel Torme (Rhino R2-71507)(Verve 823 248-2; 840 029-2)
Sarah Vaughan (Mercury 814 687-2)(Mercury 830 699-2)
Cedar Walton (Prestige OJCCD-462-2)
Gerry Wiggins (solo piano)(Concord CCD-4450)
Teddy Wilson Quintet (Black Lion BLCD-760115)
Teddy Wilson Trio (Black Lion BLCD-760184)

Tune Up (1954)

Music by Eddie Cleanhead Vinson and Miles Davis. Introduced by Miles Davis. NOTE: Duke Ellington composed a different tune titled "Tune Up" and recorded it for the SAJA label.

Monty Alexander (Concord CCD-4108)
Chet Baker (OJCCD-370-2)
Kenny Burrell/Donald Byrd (Prestige OJCCD-427-2)
Ronnie Cuber/Randy Brecker et al (PJZ CDJ-629)
Miles Davis (Natasha NI-4008)(Prestige OJCCD-093-2; 8PCD-012-2*)
Miles Davis w. Coltrane (Prestige OJCCD-128-2; 8PCD-012-2)(Yadeon 502)
Stephane Grappelli (Concord CCD-4225)
Stephane Grappelli/Vassar Clements (Flying Fish FF-70421)
Grant Green w. Sonny Clark (Mosaic MD4-133)
Bobby Hutcherson (Landmark LCD-1310-2)
Philly Joe Jones (Riverside OJCCD-230-2)
Wes Montgomery (combo)(Riverside OJCCD-089-2; 12RCD-4408-2; [alt. take] Milestone MCD-47065-2)
Wes Montgomery w. Strings (Riverside 12RCD-4408-2 [4 takes]; FCD-60-019; OJCCD-368-2; Milestone MCD-47065-2)
Sonny Rollins (Blue Note B2-84001; B2-93203)
Hilton Ruiz (Telarc CD-83338)
Sergio Salvatore (GRP GRD-9762)
Andy Simpkins Quintet (Mama Foundation 2ABASSIAJ-1)
Sonny Stitt (Muse MCD 5334)(Prestige PRCD-24127-2)(Verve 314 513 632-2)

1. Four

PLAY 5 TIMES (♩ =132)

By Miles Davis

BREAK

SOLOS

BREAK

1

2. Jeannine

PLAY 4 TIMES (♩ = 160)

By Duke Pearson

SOLOS

BRIDGE

⊕ **Ending fades out on Ab−**

3. Tune Up

PLAY 4 TIMES (♩ = 116)

By Miles Davis

Play 7 Times Then End

3

4. Perdido

By Juan Tizol

PLAY 5 TIMES (♩ = 132)

SOLOS

BRIDGE

D.C. 2nd Ending

5. Moonlight In Vermont

PLAY 3 TIMES (♩ = 60)
(NOTE: Each Chorus = 28 Measures)

By Karl Suessdorf & John Blackburn

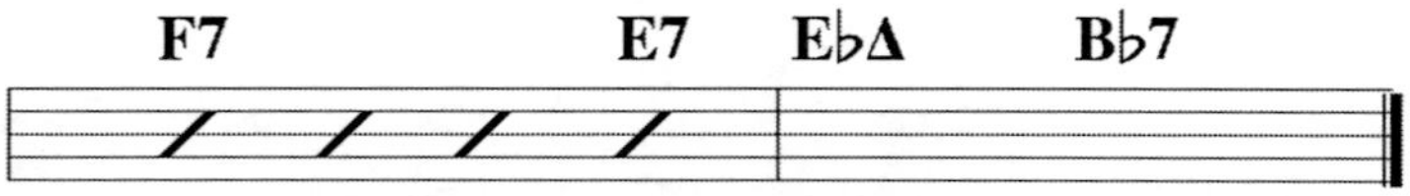

SOLOS

BRIDGE

RITARD LAST CHORUS FOR Eb△ ENDING.

6. September Song

PLAY 4 TIMES (♩ = 114)

By Kurt Weill & Maxwell Anderson

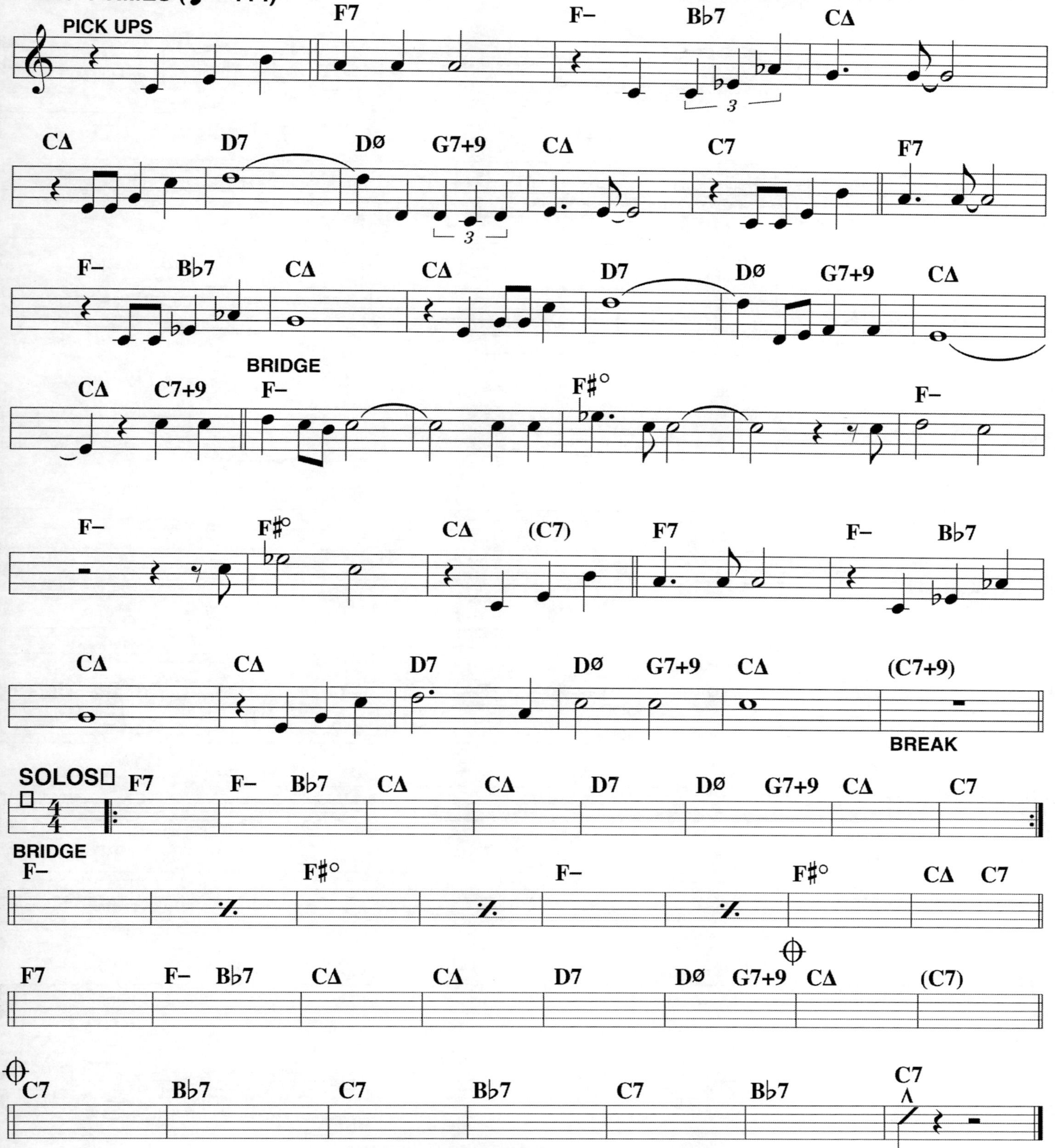

7. Fly Me To The Moon

By Bart Howard

PLAY 6 TIMES (♩ = 140)

SOLOS

PLAY 3 TIMES

BREAK

8. Nica's Dream

PLAY 3 TIMES (♩ = 112)

By Horace Silver

Nica's Dream-Cont.

SOLOS

Bb–Δ | ⁒ | Ab–Δ | ⁒

Bb–Δ | ⁒ | Ab– | Db7

Ab– | Db7 | GbΔ (Db7) | C7+9

CØ | F7+9 | Bb–Δ | ⁒

BRIDGE

Eb–/Ab | Ab7 | DbΔ | Bb7b9

Eb7 | Eb– Ab7 | DbΔ | **1.** E– A7 ‖ **2.** F7+9

Bb–Δ | ⁒ | Ab–Δ | ⁒

Bb–Δ | ⁒ | Ab– | Db7

Ab– | Db7 | GbΔ (Db7) | C7+9

CØ | F7+9 | Bb–Δ | ⁒

Bb–Δ | Ab–Δ | F#–Δ | E–Δ | CØ | F7+9 | — | Bb–Δ

BREAK

9. Along Came Betty

PLAY 4 TIMES (♩ = 116)

By Benny Golson

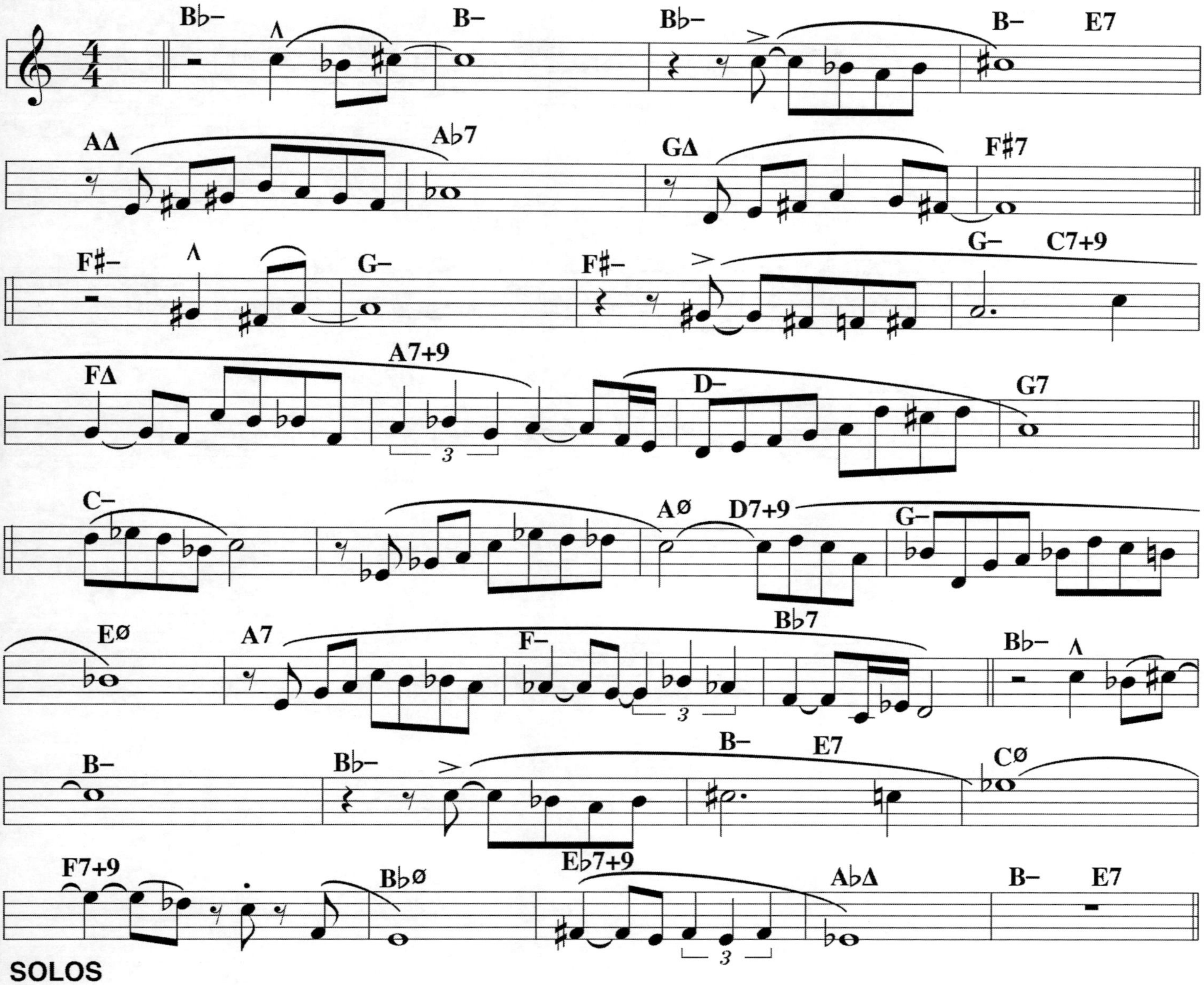

SOLOS

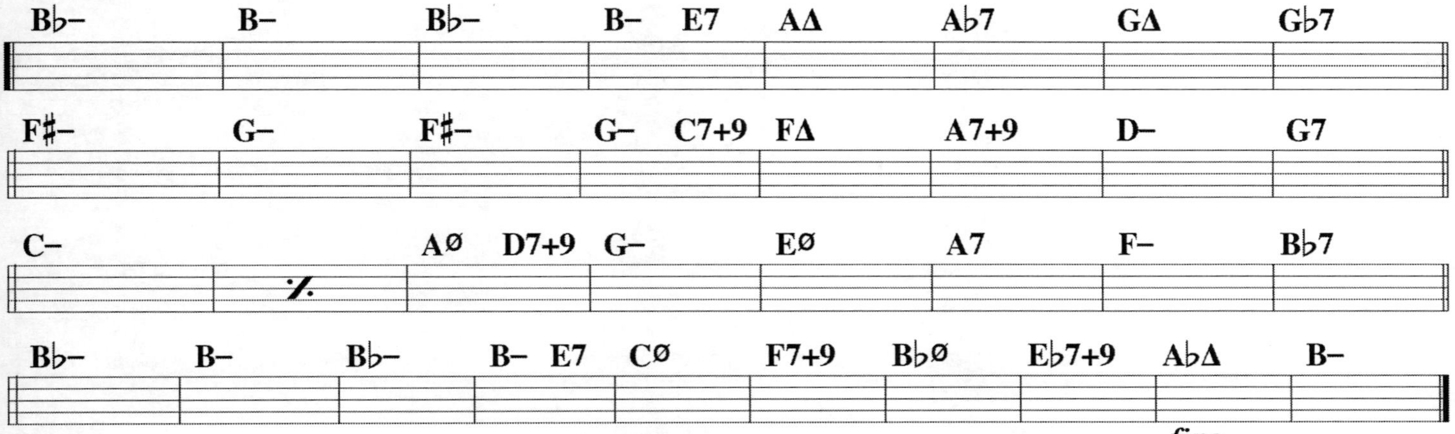

fine

10. Blues For Alice

By Charlie Parker

PLAY 10 TIMES (♩ = 108)

SOLOS

11. Good Bait

PLAY 3 TIMES (♩ = 108)

By Tadd Dameron & Count Basie

B♭Δ G– C– F7 B♭Δ G– C– F7
F– B♭7 E♭Δ A♭7 D– G7♭9 C– F7 1. B♭Δ F7
2. B♭Δ F– B♭7
BRIDGE
E♭Δ C– F– B♭7 E♭ C–
F– B♭7 E♭Δ E♭7 A♭Δ D♭7 G– C7♭9 F– B♭7♭9 E♭Δ F7
B♭Δ G– C– F7 B♭Δ G– C– F7
F– B♭7 E♭Δ A♭7 D– G7♭9 C– F7♭9 B♭Δ (F7)
SOLOS
B♭Δ G– C– F7 B♭Δ G– C– F7 B♭Δ B♭7 E♭Δ A♭7 D– G7 C– F7 B♭Δ F7
B♭Δ G– C– F7 B♭Δ G– C– F7 B♭Δ B♭7 E♭Δ A♭7 D– G7 C– F7 B♭Δ B♭7
BRIDGE
E♭Δ C– F– B♭7 E♭Δ C– F– B♭7 E♭Δ E♭7 A♭Δ D♭7 G– C7 F– B♭7 E♭Δ F7
B♭Δ G– C– F7 B♭Δ G– C– F7 B♭Δ B♭7 E♭Δ A♭7 D– G7 C– F7 B♭Δ F7
B♭ G7+9 B♭ G7 C– F7 B♭ G7+9 B♭ G7+9 C– F7 B♭

12. Take The 'A' Train

PLAY 4 TIMES (♩ = 112)

By Billy Strayhorn

INTRO

MELODY

1. CΔ   2. CΔ

BRIDGE

SOLOS

BRIDGE

13. Bye, Bye Blackbird

PLAY 6 TIMES (♩ = 138)

By Mort Dixon & Ray Henderson

SOLOS

Play 4 Times

BREAK

14. Speak Low

By Kurt Weill & Ogden Nash

PLAY 3 TIMES (♩ = 116)

15

15. But Not For Me

PLAY 4 TIMES (♩ = 150)

By George Gershwin & Ira Gershwin

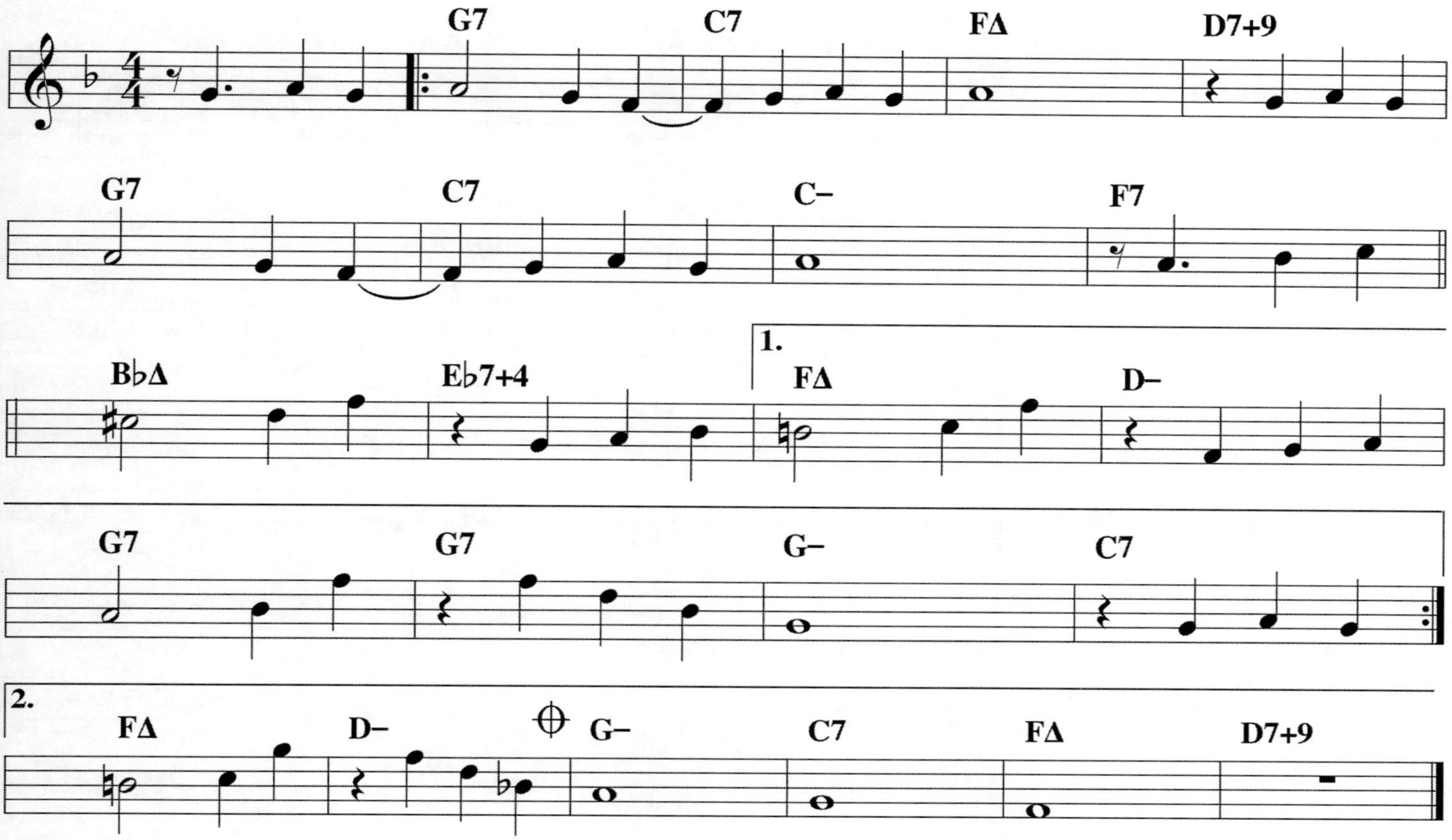
G7
C7
FΔ
D7+9
G7
C7
C–
F7
B♭Δ
E♭7+4
1.
FΔ
D–
G7
G7
G–
C7
2.
FΔ
D–
G–
C7
FΔ
D7+9

SOLOS

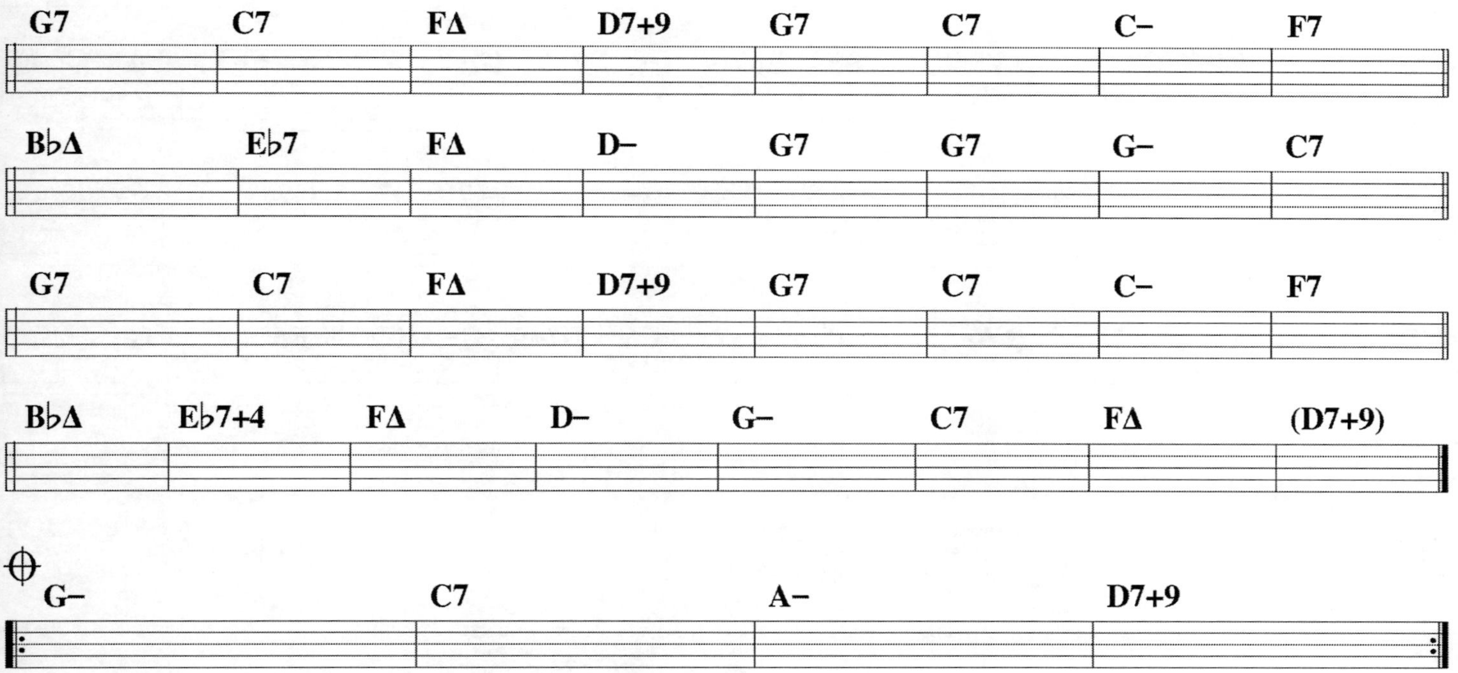
G7
C7
FΔ
D7+9
G7
C7
C–
F7
B♭Δ
E♭7
FΔ
D–
G7
G7
G–
C7
G7
C7
FΔ
D7+9
G7
C7
C–
F7
B♭Δ
E♭7+4
FΔ
D–
G–
C7
FΔ
(D7+9)
G–
C7
A–
D7+9

16. Mean To Me

By Fred E. Ahlert & Roy Turk

PLAY 3 TIMES (♩ = 104)

17. Confirmation

PLAY 5 TIMES (♩ = 116)

By Charlie Parker

fine = **F7+4**

18. Oleo

PLAY 8 TIMES (♩ =200)

By Miles Davis

19. Moment's Notice

PLAY 6 TIMES (♩ = 176)

By John Coltrane

20. Stablemates

(The form in measures = 14–8–14)

By Benny Golson

PLAY 4 TIMES (♩ = 112)

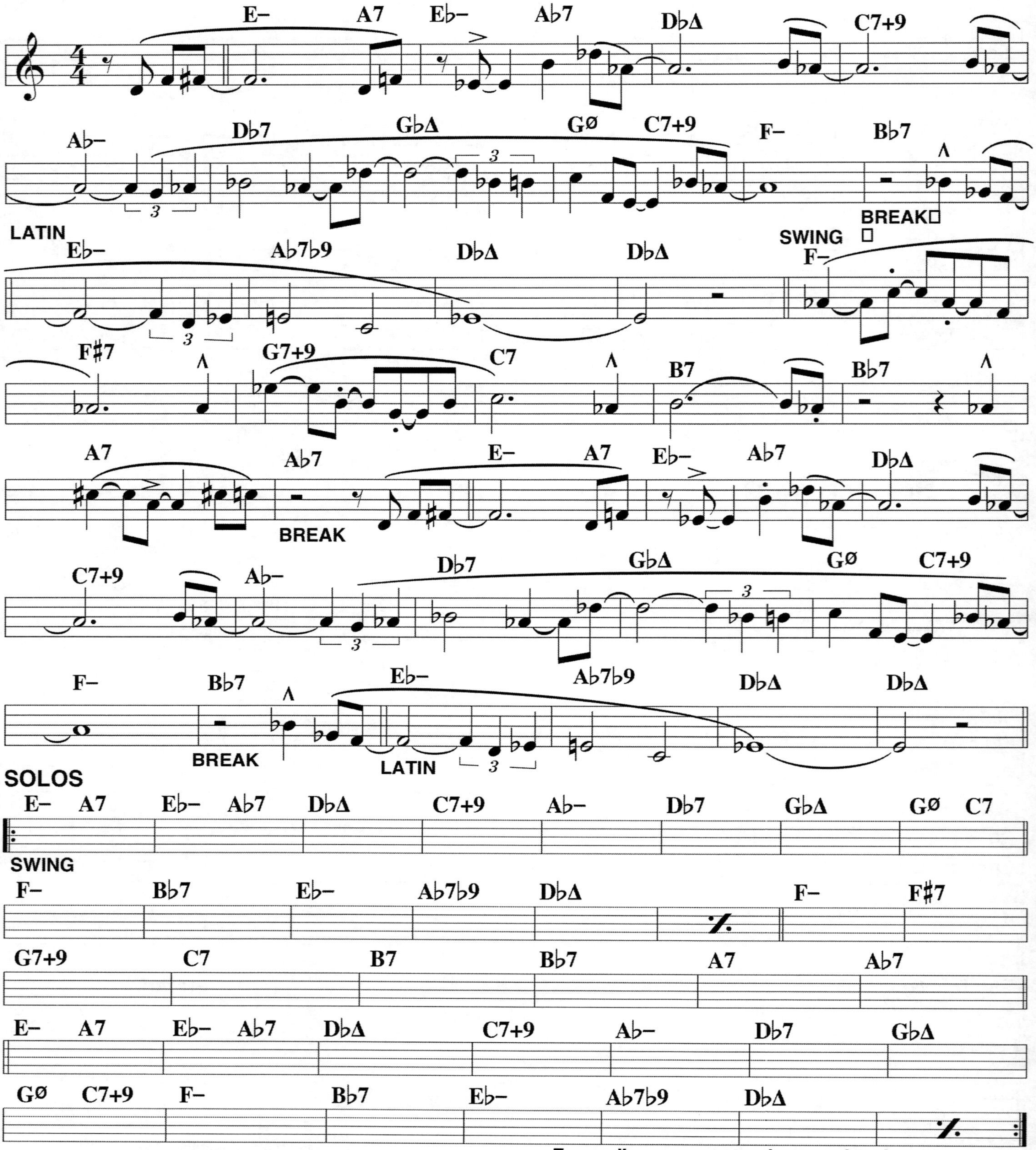
E– A7 Eb– Ab7 DbΔ C7+9
Ab– Db7 GbΔ GØ C7+9 F– Bb7
BREAK
LATIN
Eb– Ab7b9 DbΔ DbΔ
SWING
F–
F#7 G7+9 C7 B7 Bb7
A7 Ab7 E– A7 Eb– Ab7 DbΔ
BREAK
C7+9 Ab– Db7 GbΔ GØ C7+9
F– Bb7 Eb– Ab7b9 DbΔ DbΔ
BREAK
LATIN
SOLOS
E– A7 Eb– Ab7 DbΔ C7+9 Ab– Db7 GbΔ GØ C7
SWING
F– Bb7 Eb– Ab7b9 DbΔ F– F#7
G7+9 C7 B7 Bb7 A7 Ab7
E– A7 Eb– Ab7 DbΔ C7+9 Ab– Db7 GbΔ
GØ C7+9 F– Bb7 Eb– Ab7b9 DbΔ

For ending, repeat two times and end.

21. Algo Bueno

By Dizzy Gillespie

PLAY 4 TIMES (♩ = 142)

The melody has been altered 1/2 step in bars 2 & 6 of the bridge to conform to the altered changes jazz players usually play.

SOLOS

22. Giant Steps

PLAY 11 TIMES (♩ = 110) (Bossa Nova)
PLAY 9 TIMES (♩ = 120) (Swing)

By John Coltrane

NOTE: One recorded version is "Bossa Nova" and the other is "Swing"

BΔ   D7   GΔ   Bb7   EbΔ   A−   D7

GΔ   Bb7   EbΔ   F#7   BΔ   F−   Bb7   EbΔ

EbΔ   A−   D7   GΔ   C#−   F#7   BΔ

BΔ   F−   Bb7   EbΔ   C#−   F#7

SOLOS

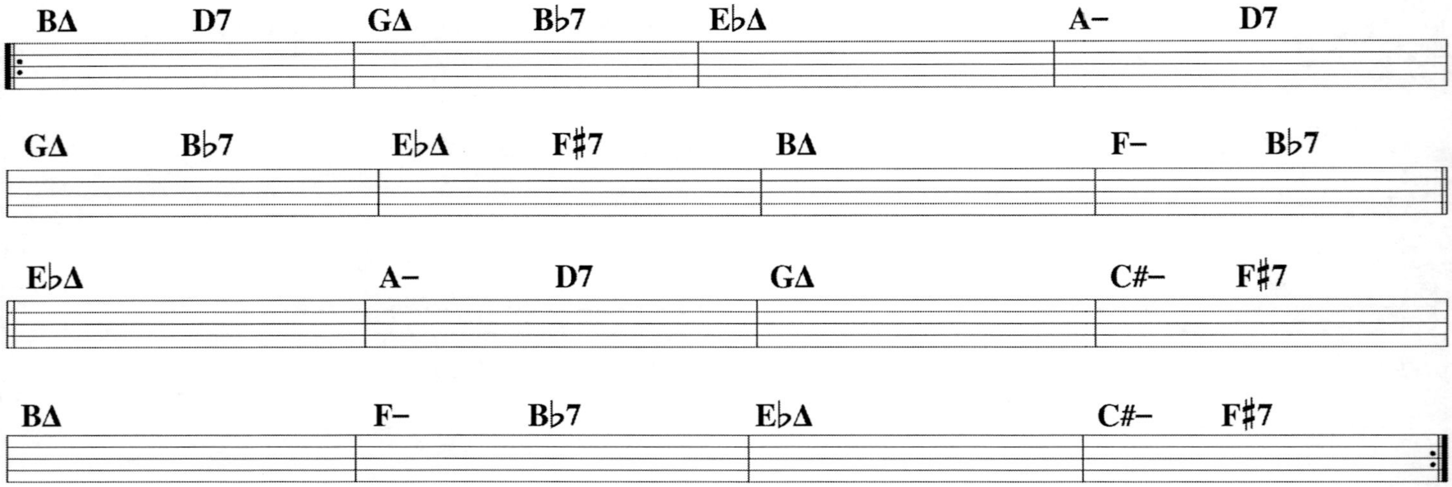

BΔ   D7   GΔ   Bb7   EbΔ   A−   D7

GΔ   Bb7   EbΔ   F#7   BΔ   F−   Bb7

EbΔ   A−   D7   GΔ   C#−   F#7

BΔ   F−   Bb7   EbΔ   C#−   F#7

fine

1. Four

By Miles Davis

PLAY 5 TIMES (♩ = 132)

BREAK

SOLOS

BREAK

2. Jeannine

By Duke Pearson

PLAY 4 TIMES (♩ = 160)

SOLOS

BRIDGE

⊕ **Ending fades out on Bb–**

25

B♭ B♭

3. Tune Up

PLAY 4 TIMES (♩ = 116)

By Miles Davis

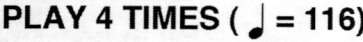

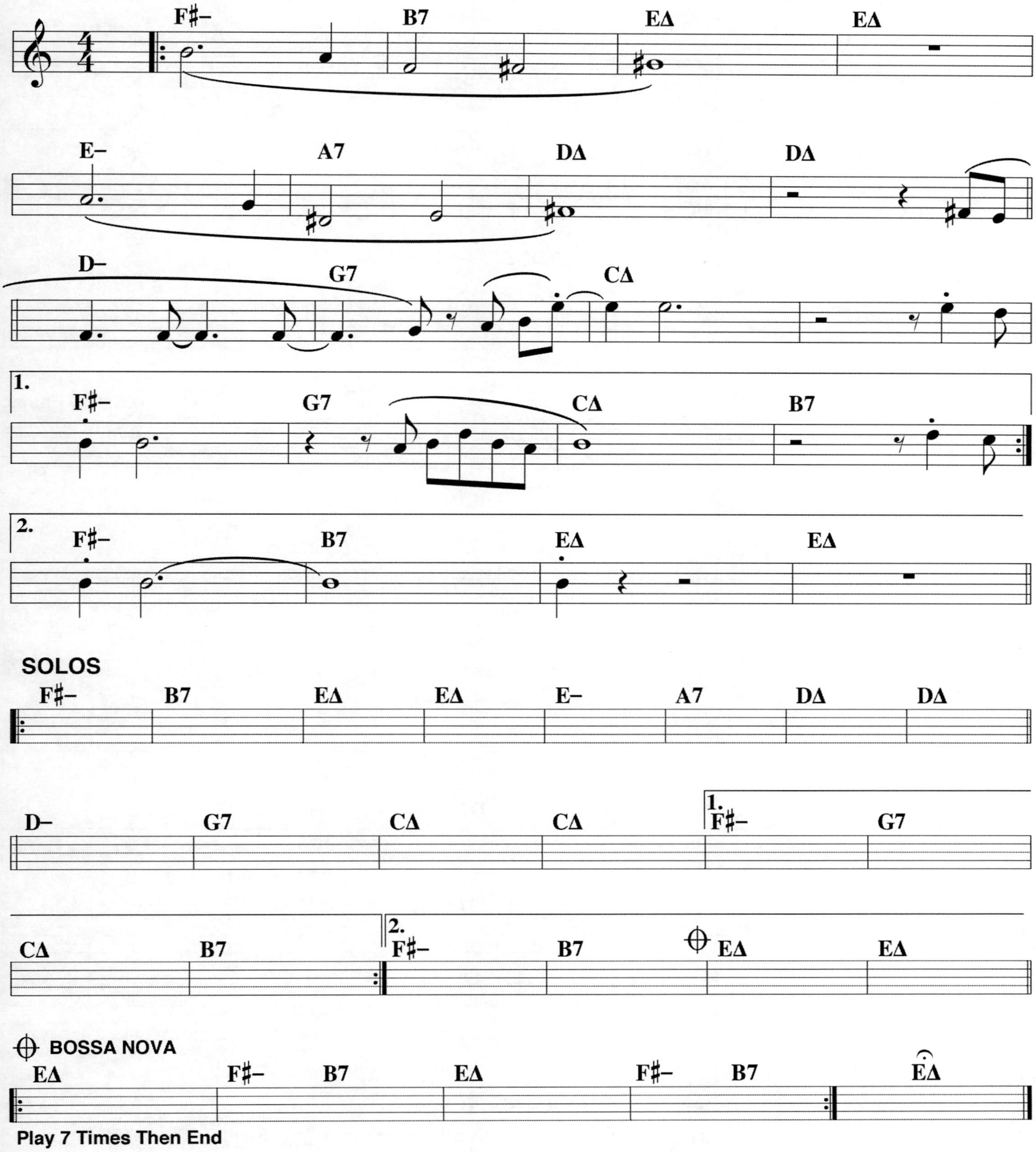

B♭ B♭

4. Perdido

By Juan Tizol

PLAY 5 TIMES (♩ = 132)

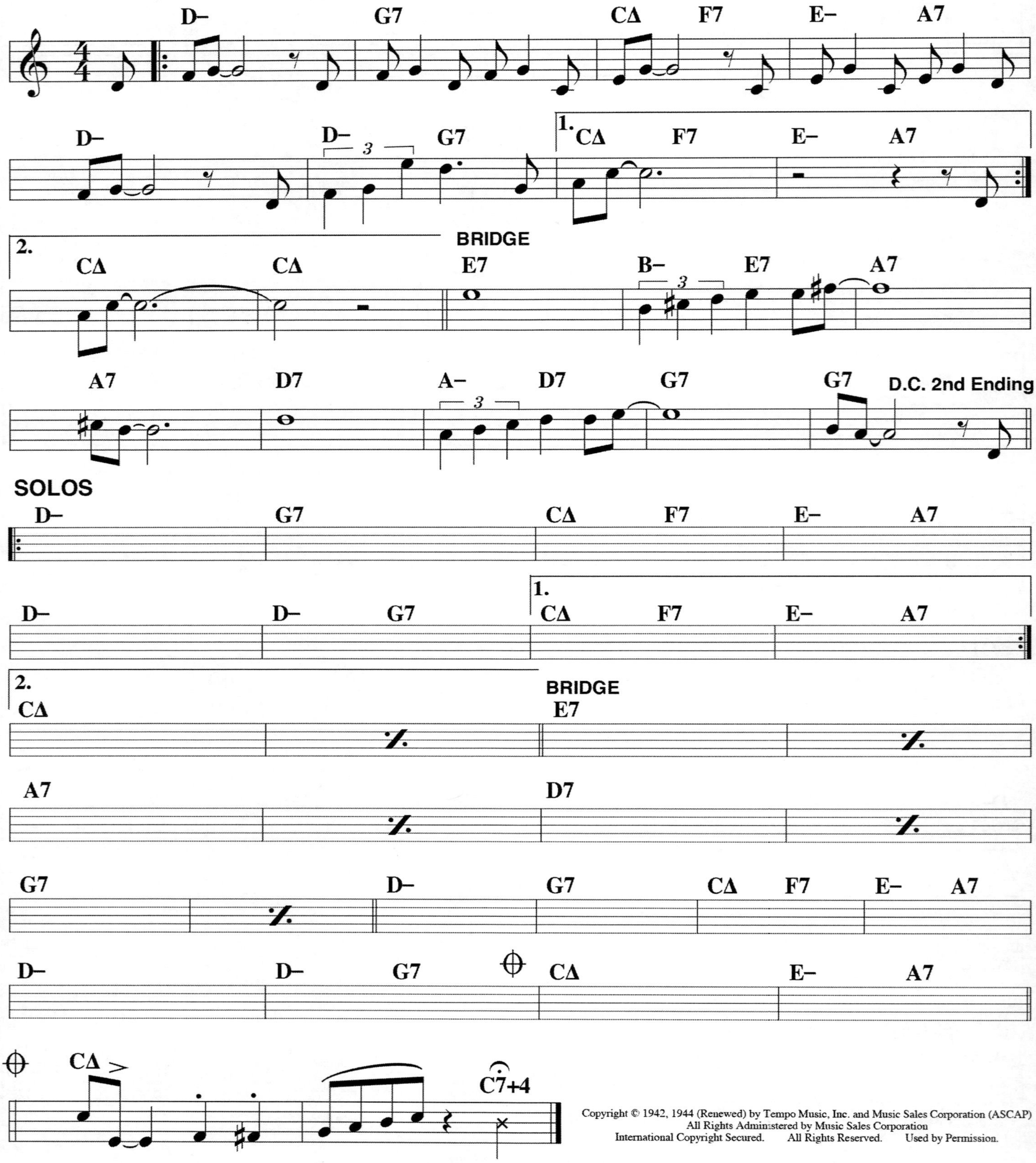

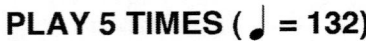

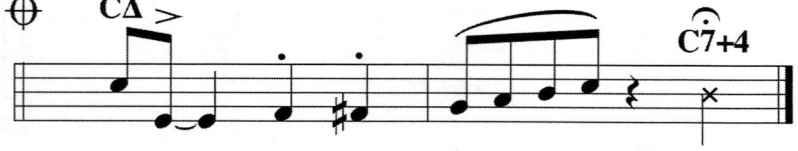

5. Moonlight In Vermont

PLAY 3 TIMES (♩ = 60)
(NOTE: Each Chorus = 28 Measures)

By Karl Suessdorf & John Blackburn

SOLOS

BRIDGE

RITARD LAST CHORUS FOR FΔ ENDING.

6. September Song

By Kurt Weill & Maxwell Anderson

PLAY 4 TIMES (♩ = 114)

29

7. Fly Me To The Moon

By Bart Howard

PLAY 6 TIMES (♩ = 140)

SOLOS

PLAY 3 TIMES

BREAK

8. Nica's Dream

PLAY 3 TIMES (♩ = 112)

By Horace Silver

BRIDGE

Nica's Dream-Cont.

9. Along Came Betty

By Benny Golson

PLAY 4 TIMES (♩ = 116)

SOLOS

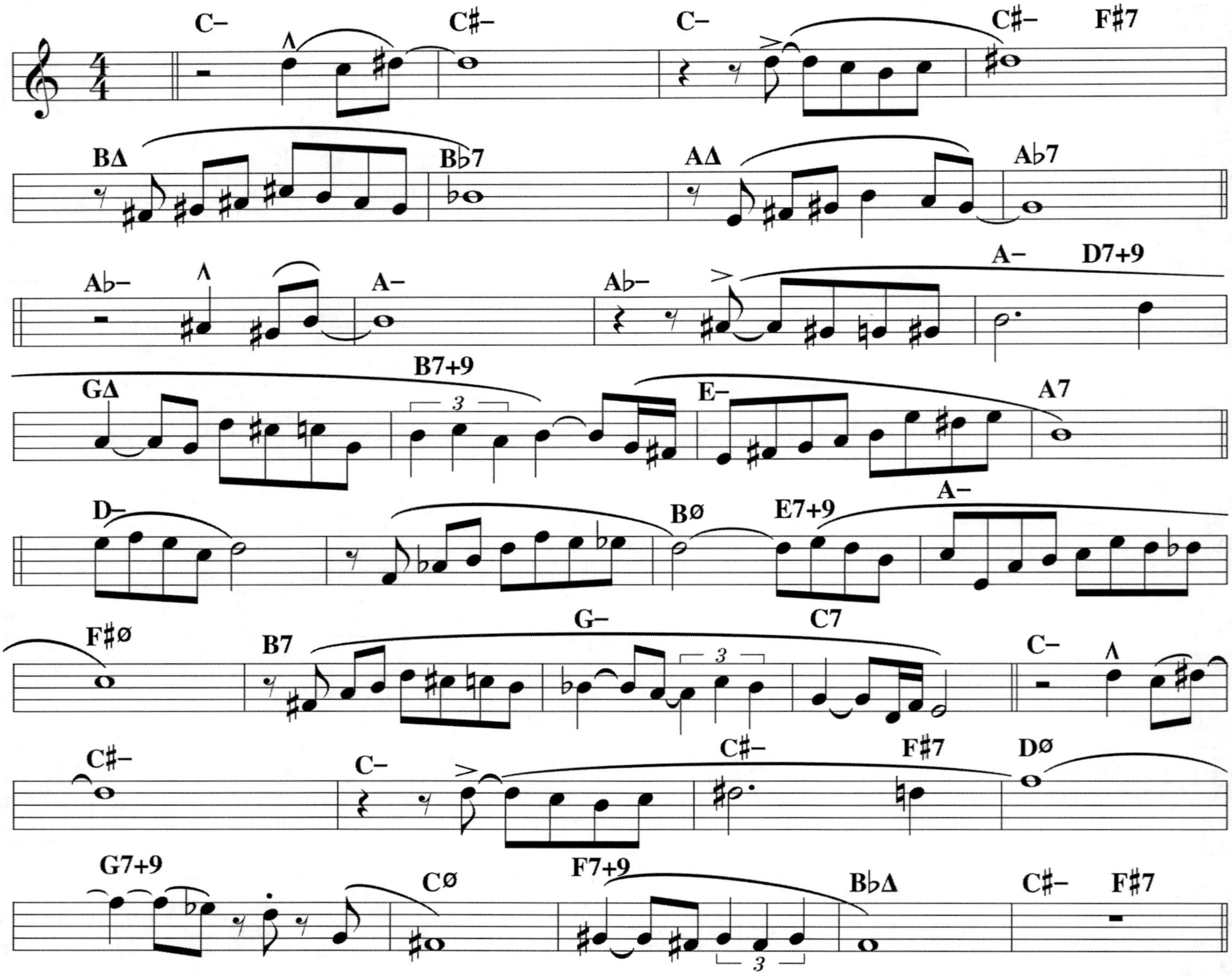

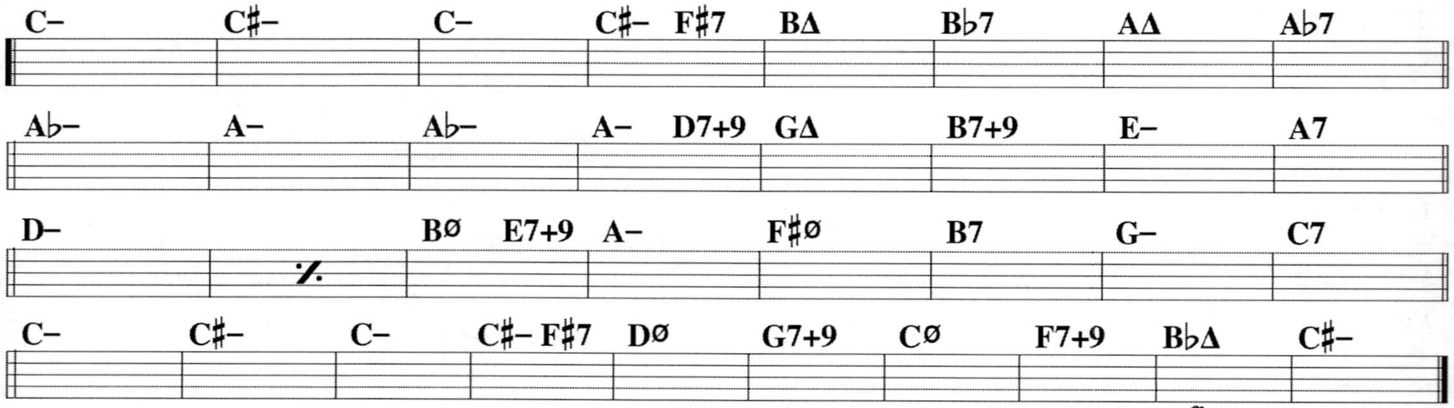

C−	C♯−	C−	C♯− F♯7	B△	B♭7	A△	A♭7

A♭−	A−	A♭−	A− D7+9 G△	B7+9	E−	A7

D−		℀	B∅ E7+9 A−	F♯∅	B7	G−	C7

C−	C♯−	C−	C♯− F♯7 D∅	G7+9	C∅	F7+9	B♭△	C♯−

fine

10. Blues For Alice

B♭

By Charlie Parker

PLAY 10 TIMES (♩ = 108)

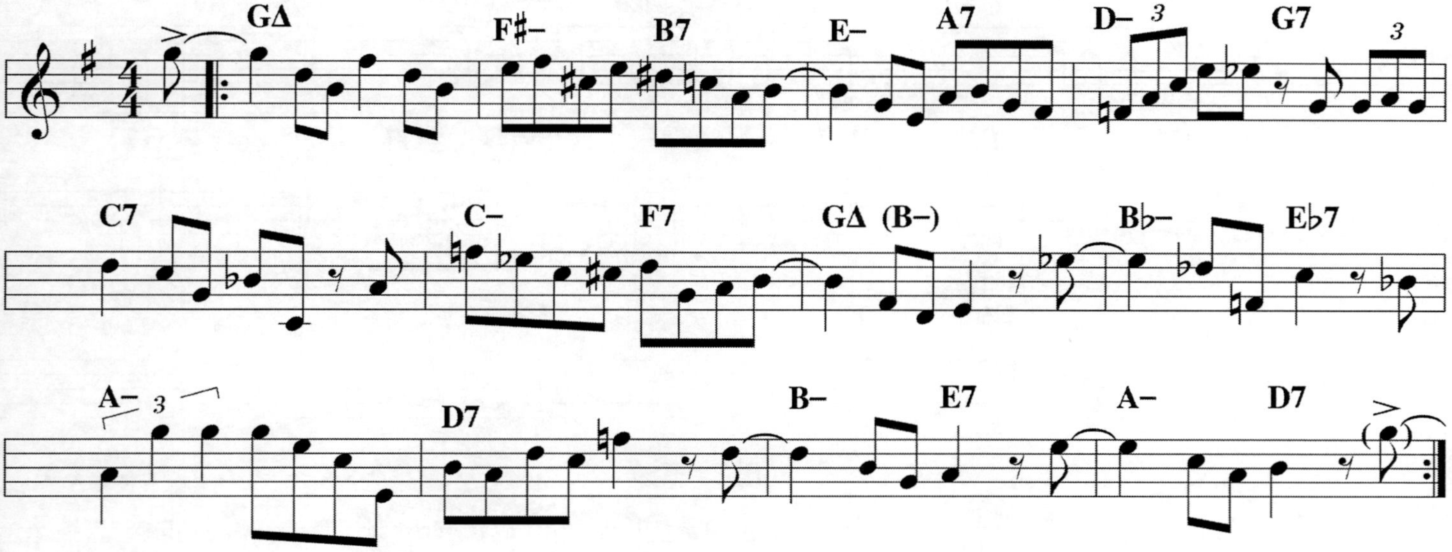

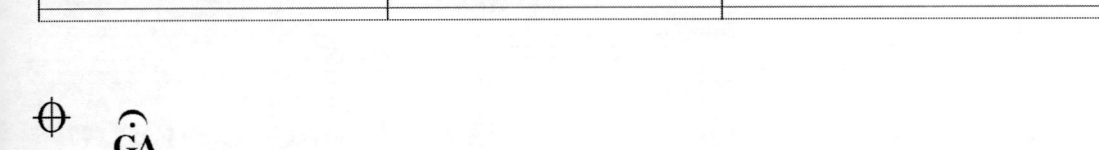

SOLOS

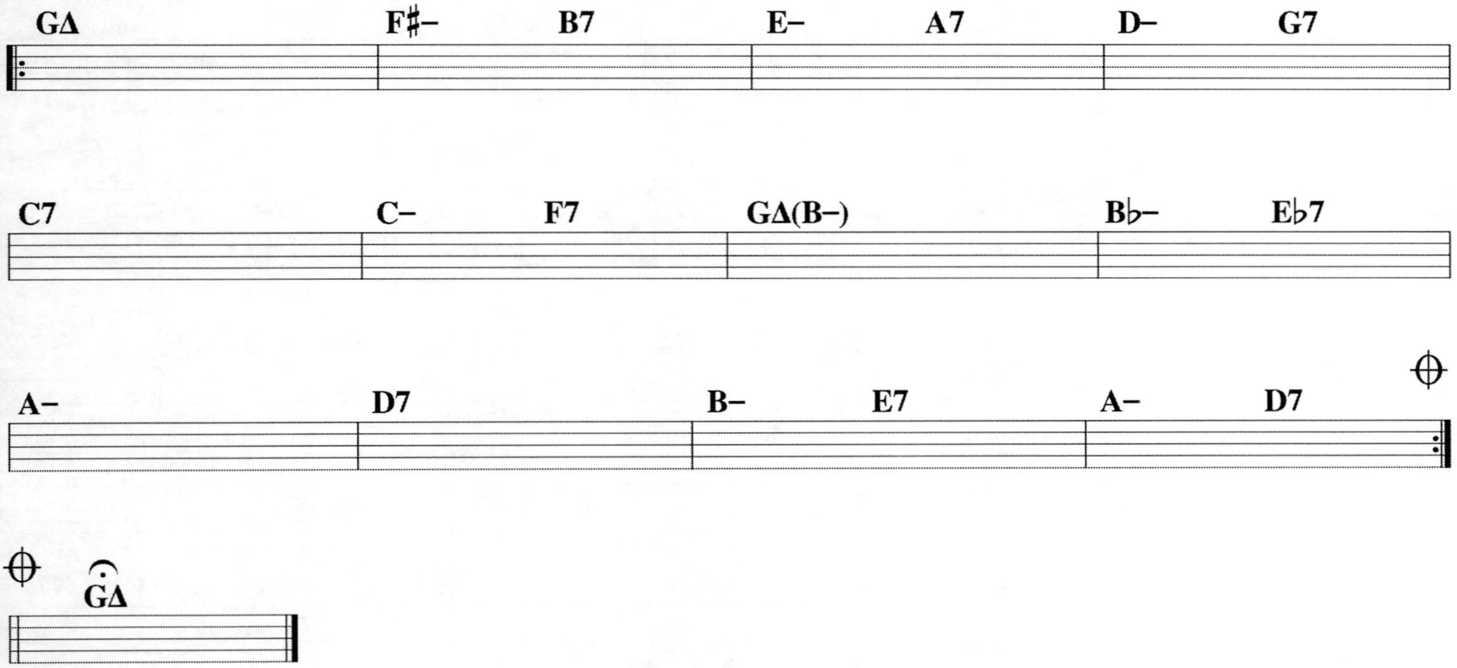

11. Good Bait

B♭ B♭

By Tadd Dameron & Count Basie

PLAY 3 TIMES (♩ = 108)

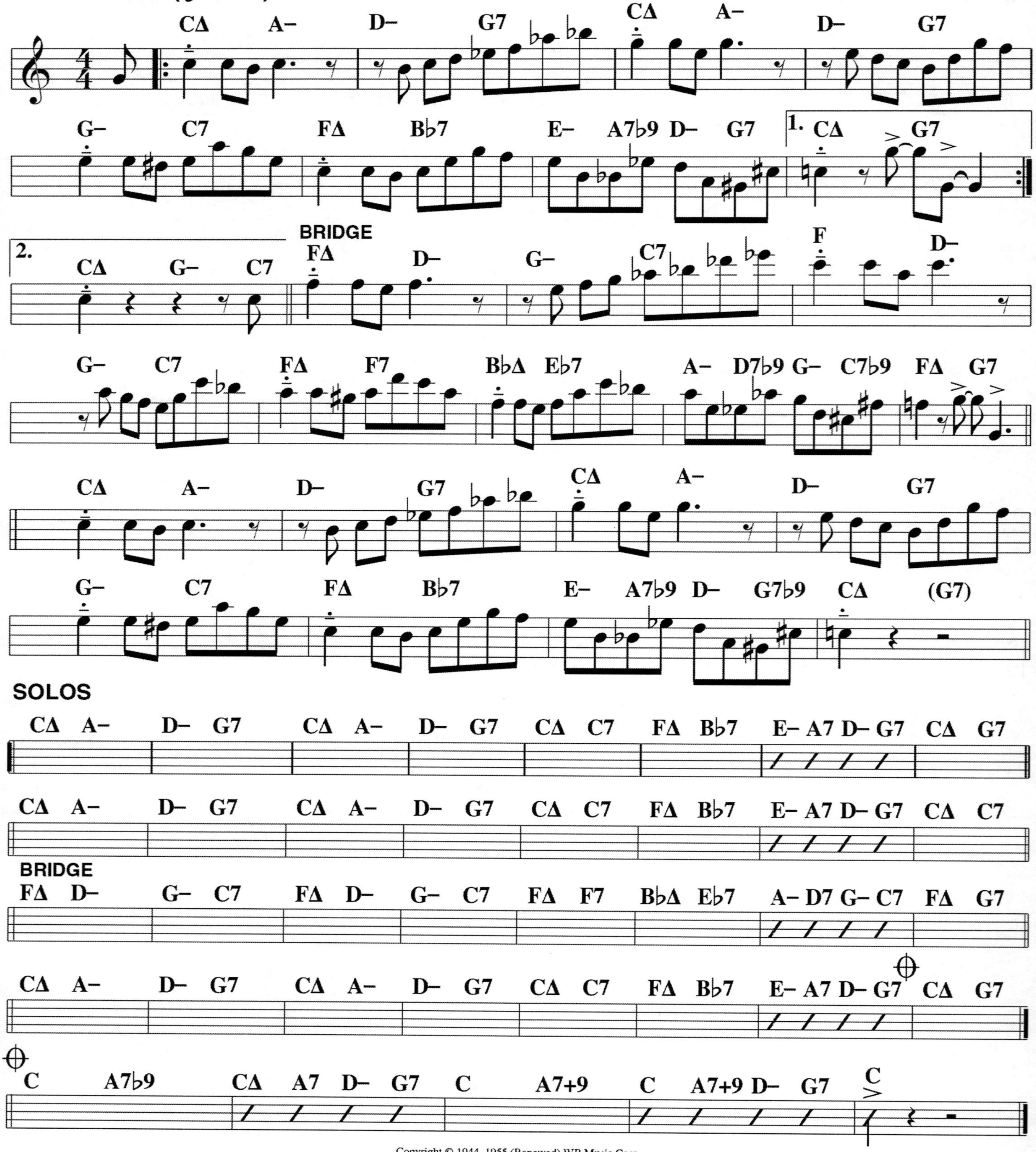

12. Take The 'A' Train

PLAY 4 TIMES (♩ = 112)

By Billy Strayhorn

INTRO (PIANO CUES-2X)

MELODY

SOLOS

BRIDGE

13. Bye, Bye Blackbird

By Mort Dixon & Ray Henderson

PLAY 6 TIMES (♩ = 138)

SOLOS

Play 4 Times

BREAK

Copyright © 1926 (Renewed) Warner Bros. Inc.
WARNER BROS. PUBLICATIONS U.S. INC
International Copyright Secured.   All Rights Reserved.   Used by Permission.

37

14. Speak Low

By Kurt Weill & Ogden Nash

PLAY 3 TIMES (♩ = 116)

SOLOS

BRIDGE

Repeat & Fade Out

15. But Not For Me

B♭

By George Gershwin & Ira Gershwin

PLAY 4 TIMES (♩ = 150)

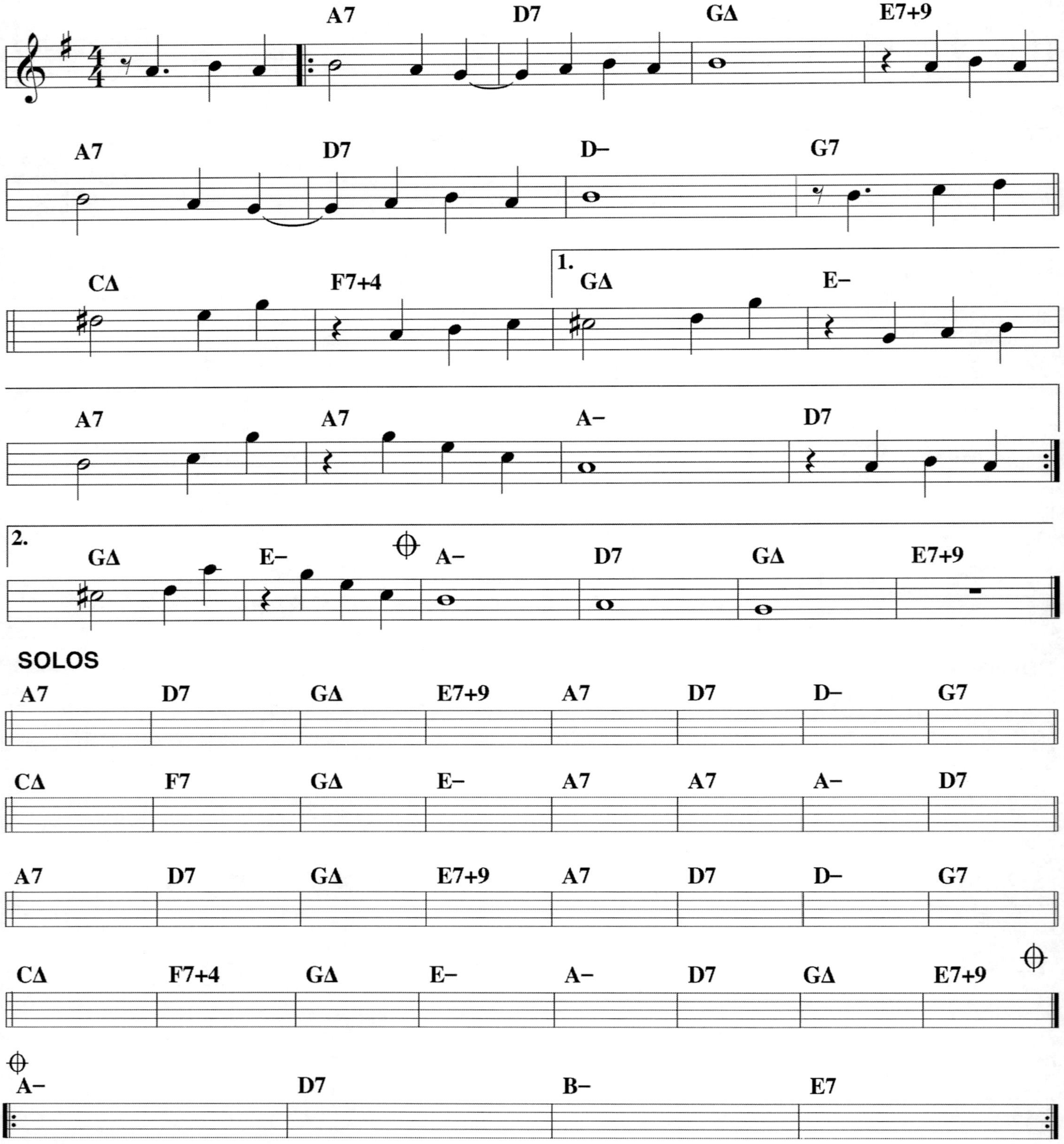
A7
D7
GΔ
E7+9
A7
D7
D–
G7
CΔ
F7+4
1.
GΔ
E–
A7
A7
A–
D7
2.
GΔ
E–
A–
D7
GΔ
E7+9
SOLOS
A7 D7 GΔ E7+9 A7 D7 D– G7
CΔ F7 GΔ E– A7 A7 A– D7
A7 D7 GΔ E7+9 A7 D7 D– G7
CΔ F7+4 GΔ E– A– D7 GΔ E7+9
A– D7 B– E7

Repeat Over & Over & Fade Out

16. Mean To Me

By Fred E. Ahlert & Roy Turk

PLAY 3 TIMES (♩ = 104)

SOLOS

BRIDGE

17. Confirmation

By Charlie Parker

PLAY 5 TIMES (♩ = 116)

fine = G7+4

B♭ B♭

18. Oleo

PLAY 8 TIMES (♩ =200)

By Miles Davis

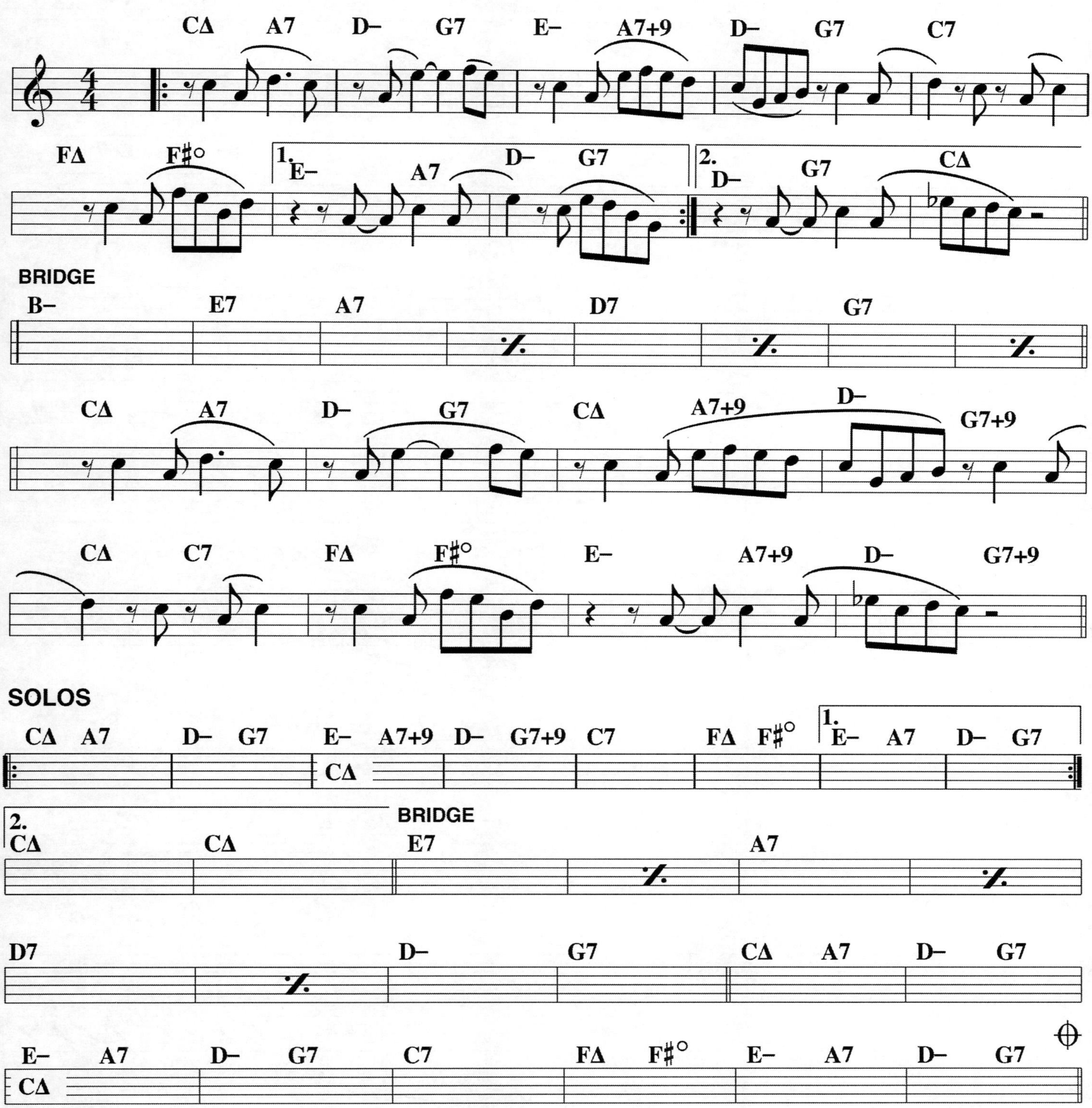

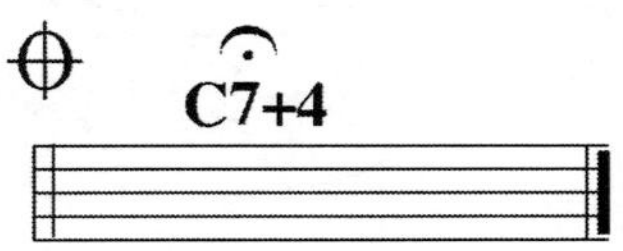

19. Moment's Notice

43

20. Stablemates

(The form in measures = 14–8–14)

By Benny Golson

PLAY 4 TIMES (♩ = 112)

SOLOS

| F#– | B7 | F– | Bb7 | EbΔ | | D7+9 | Bb– | Eb7 | AbΔ | | Aø | D7 |

SWING

| G– | | C7 | | F– | | Bb7b9 | EbΔ | | | | G– | | Ab7 |

| A7+9 | | D7 | | C#7 | | C7 | | B7 | | Bb7 |

| F#– | B7 | F– | Bb7 | EbΔ | | D7+9 | Bb– | Eb7 | AbΔ |

| Aø | D7+9 | G– | | C7 | | F– | | Bb7b9 | EbΔ | | |

For ending, repeat two times and end.

21. Algo Bueno

By Dizzy Gillespie

PLAY 4 TIMES (♩ = 142)

The melody has been altered 1/2 step in bars 2 & 6 of the bridge to conform to the altered changes jazz players usually play.

SOLOS

| A∅ | D7+9 | G∅ | C7+9 | F∅ | Bb7+9 | EbΔ | EbΔ |

BRIDGE

| Bb− | | B− | E7 | Bb− | Eb7 | AbΔ | |

| C− | | C#− | F#7 | C− | F7 | Bb7 | |

| A∅ | D7+9 | G∅ | C7+99 | F∅ | Bb7+9 | ⊕ EbΔ | EbΔ |

⊕

| EbΔ | F− | EbΔ | F− | EbΔ | F− | EbΔ | EbΔ+4 |

B♭ B♭

22. Giant Steps

PLAY 11 TIMES (♩ = 110) (Bossa Nova)
PLAY 9 TIMES (♩ = 120) (Swing)

By John Coltrane

NOTE: One recorded version is "Bossa Nova" and the other is "Swing"

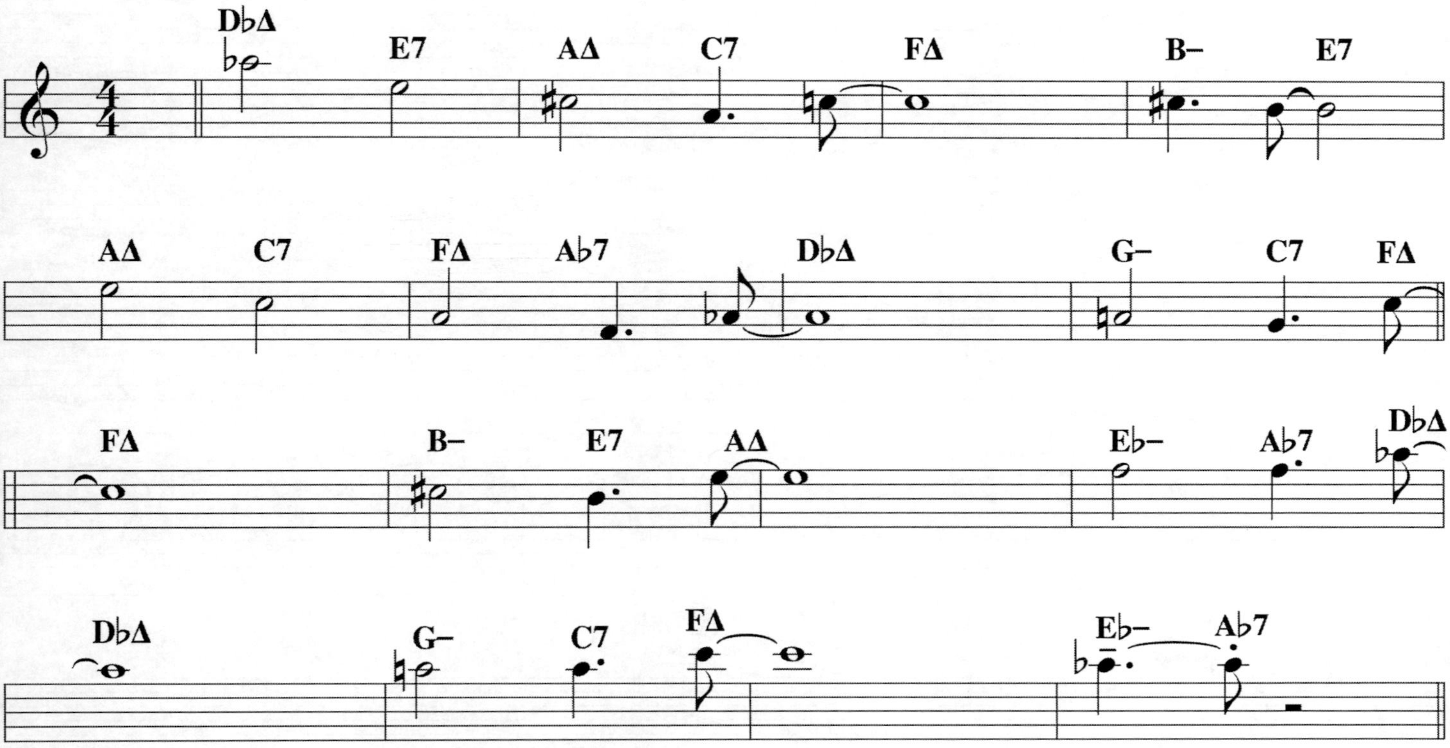

SOLOS

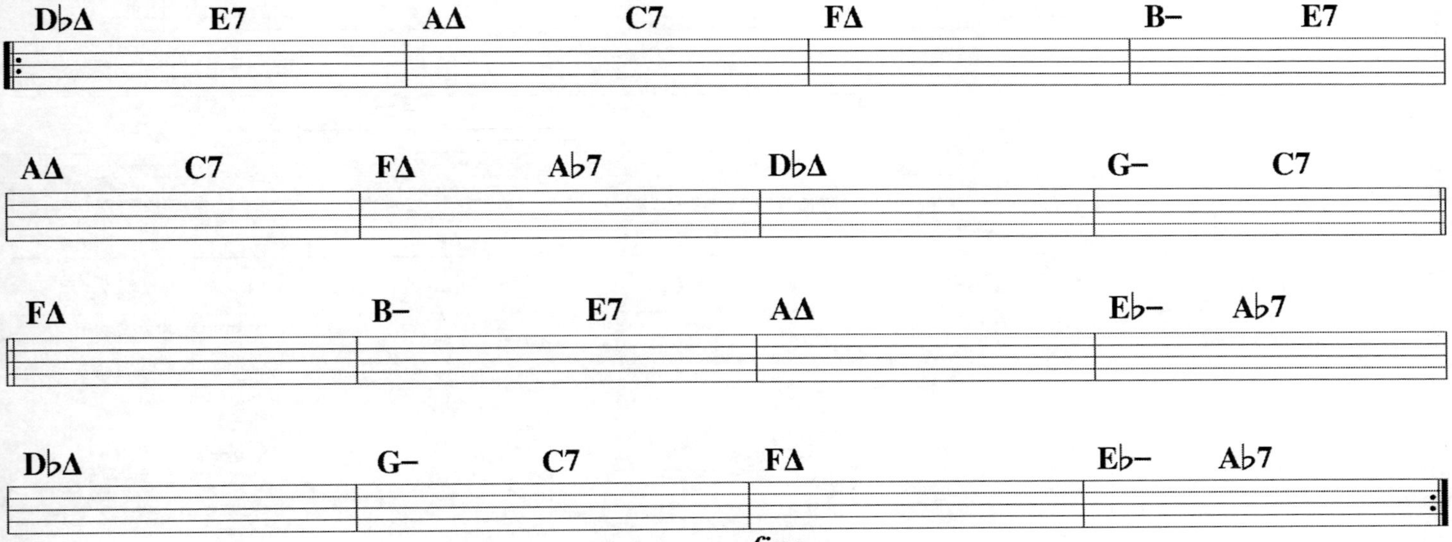

fine

1. Four

Eb

Eb

By Miles Davis

PLAY 5 TIMES (♩ = 132)

SOLOS

BREAK

2. Jeannine

3. Tune Up

PLAY 4 TIMES (♩ = 116)

By Miles Davis

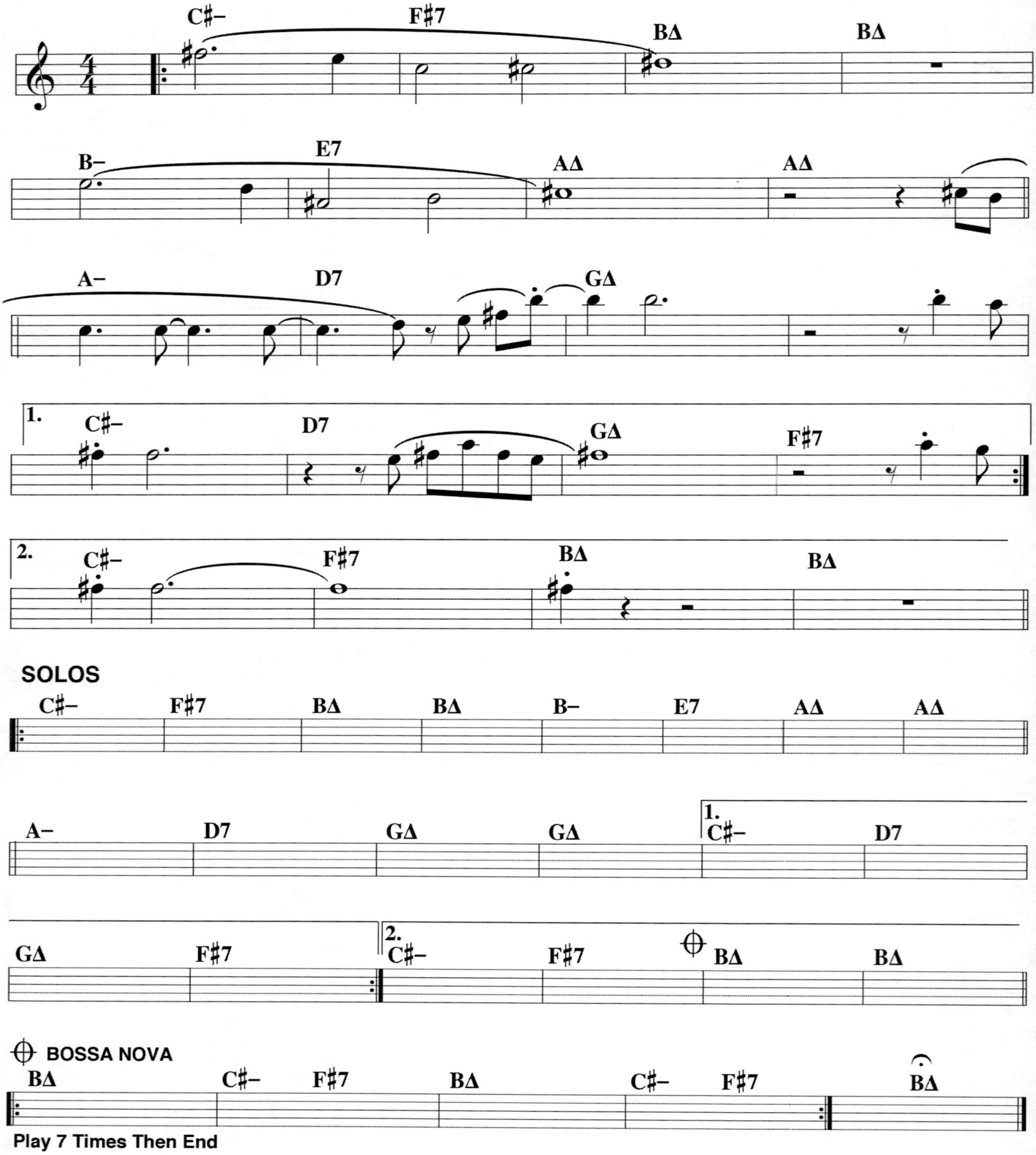

SOLOS

| C#− | F#7 | BΔ | BΔ | B− | E7 | AΔ | AΔ |

| A− | D7 | GΔ | GΔ | **1.** C#− | D7 |

| GΔ | F#7 | **2.** C#− | F#7 | ⊕ BΔ | BΔ |

⊕ BOSSA NOVA

| BΔ | C#− | F#7 | BΔ | C#− | F#7 | BΔ |

Play 7 Times Then End

4. Perdido

By Juan Tizol

5. Moonlight In Vermont

PLAY 3 TIMES (♩ = 60)
(NOTE: Each Chorus = 28 Measures)

By Karl Suessdorf & John Blackburn

SOLOS

BRIDGE

RITARD LAST CHORUS FOR CΔ ENDING.

Eb

6. September Song

Eb

By Kurt Weill & Maxwell Anderson

PLAY 4 TIMES (♩ = 114)

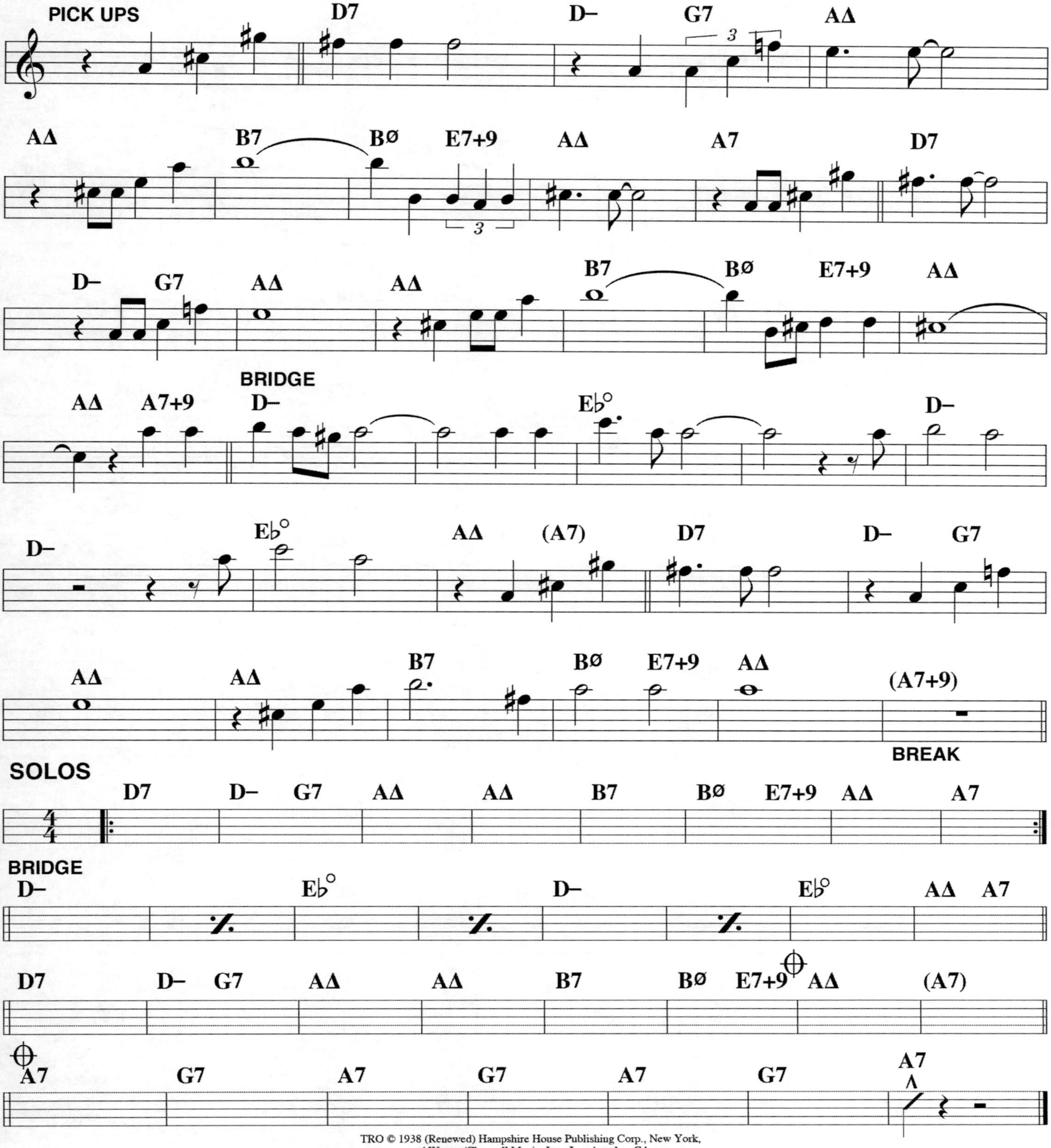

7. Fly Me To The Moon

By Bart Howard

PLAY 6 TIMES (♩ = 140)

SOLOS

PLAY 3 TIMES

BREAK

Eb

8. Nica's Dream

Eb

PLAY 3 TIMES (♩ = 112)

By Horace Silver

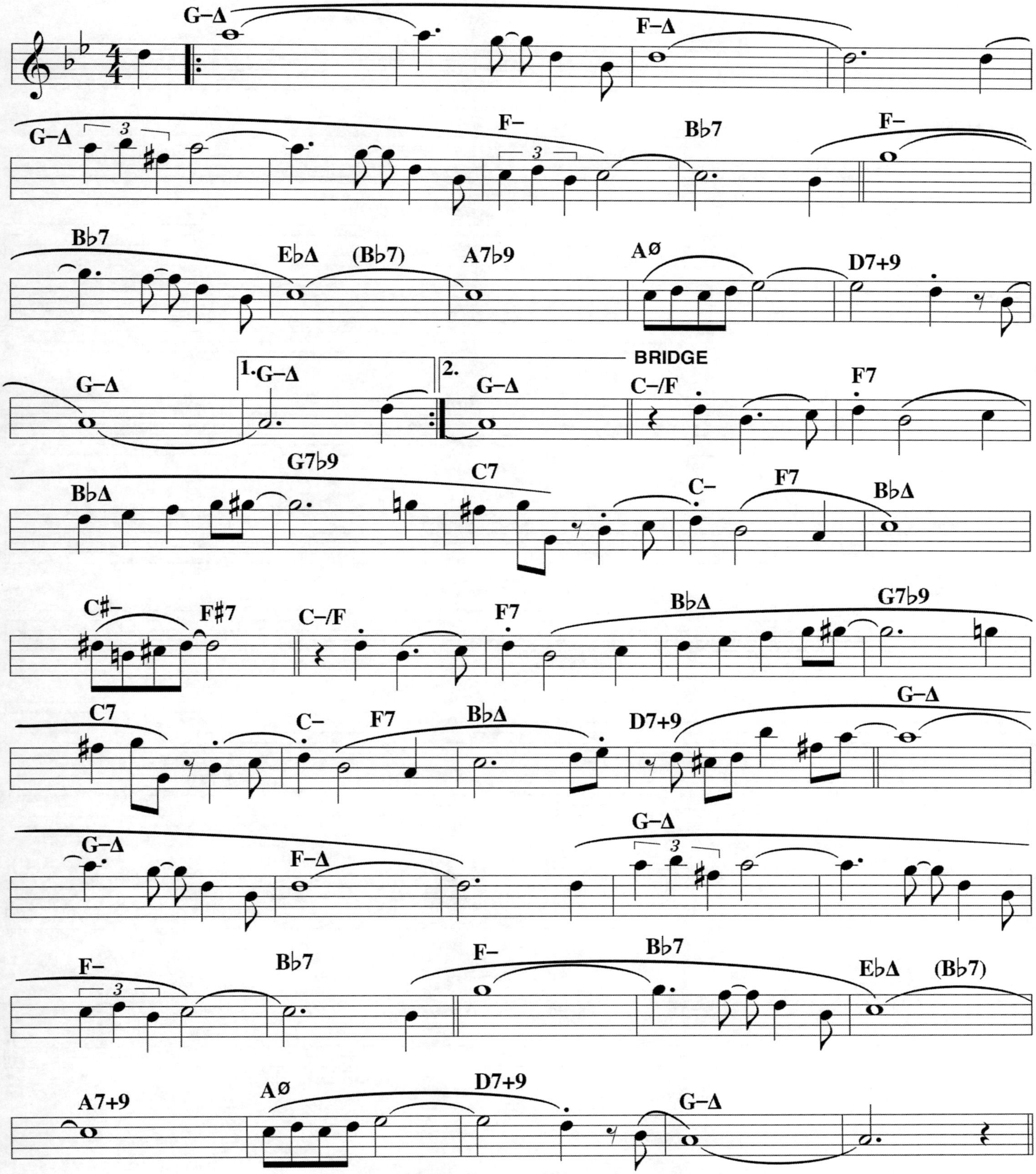

Nica's Dream-Cont.

55

9. Along Came Betty

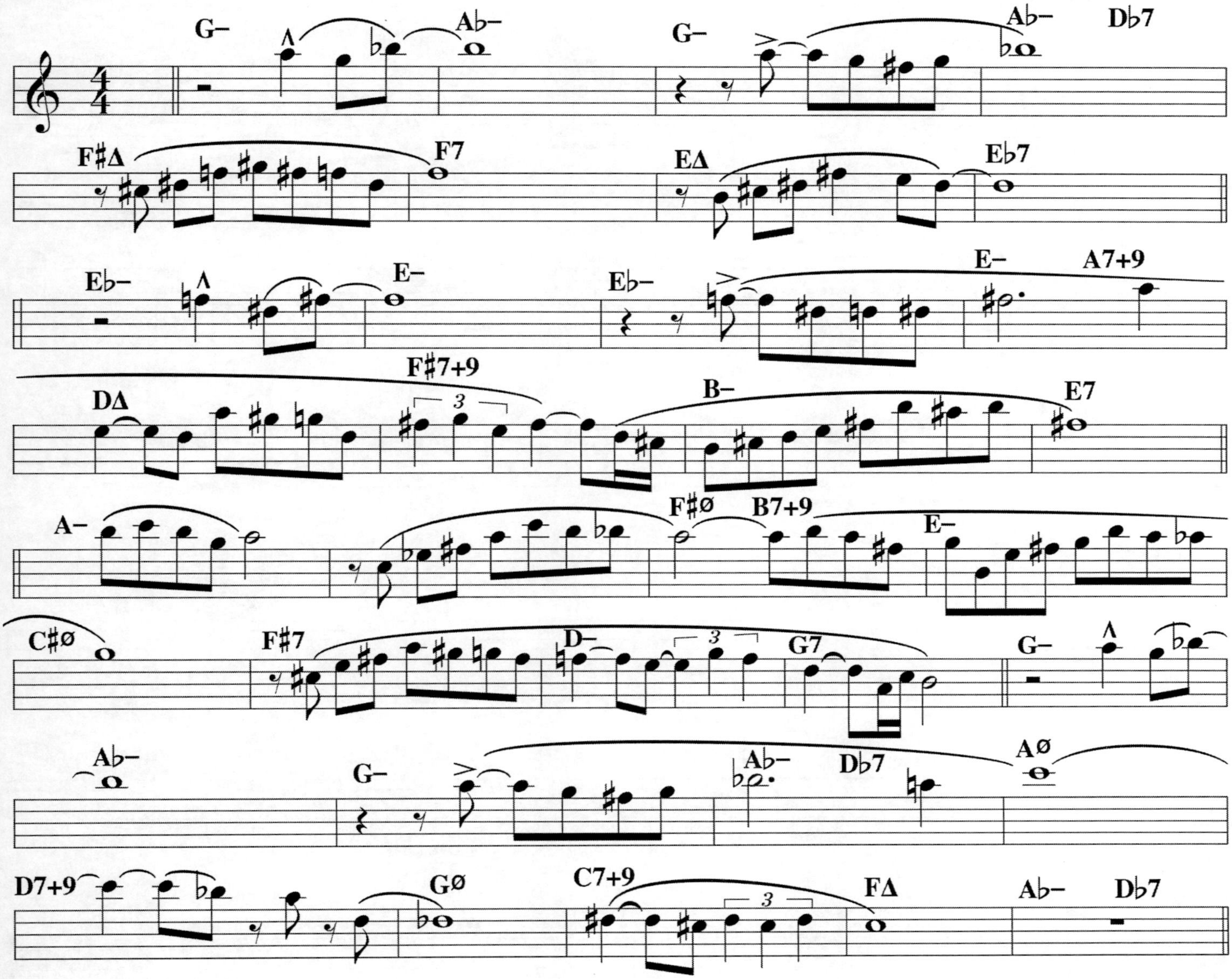

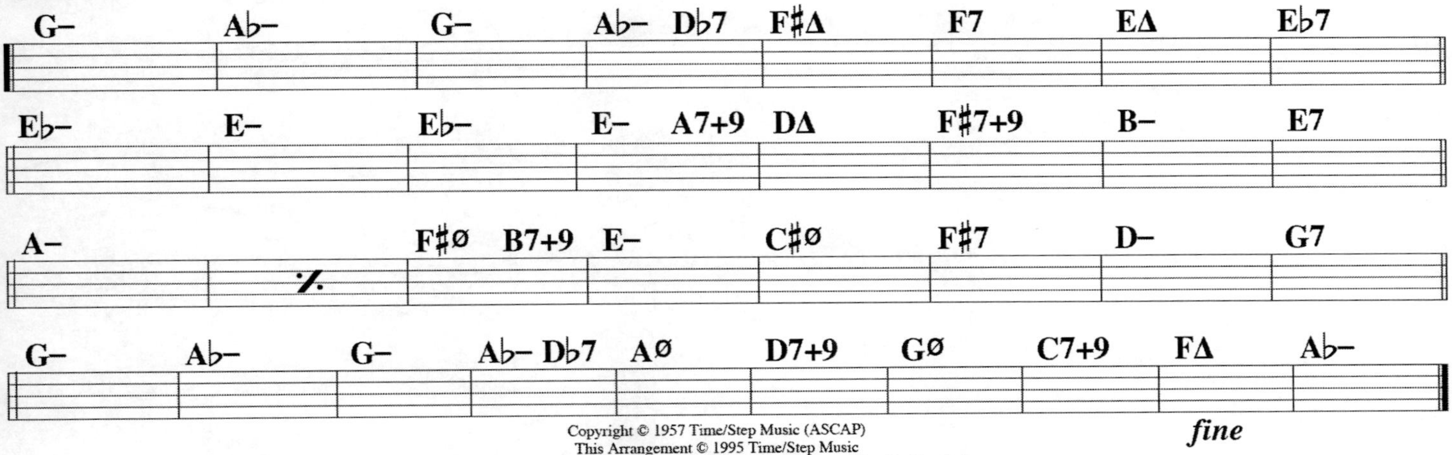

By Benny Golson

PLAY 4 TIMES (♩ = 116)

fine

10. Blues For Alice

E♭ E♭

By Charlie Parker

PLAY 10 TIMES (♩ = 108)

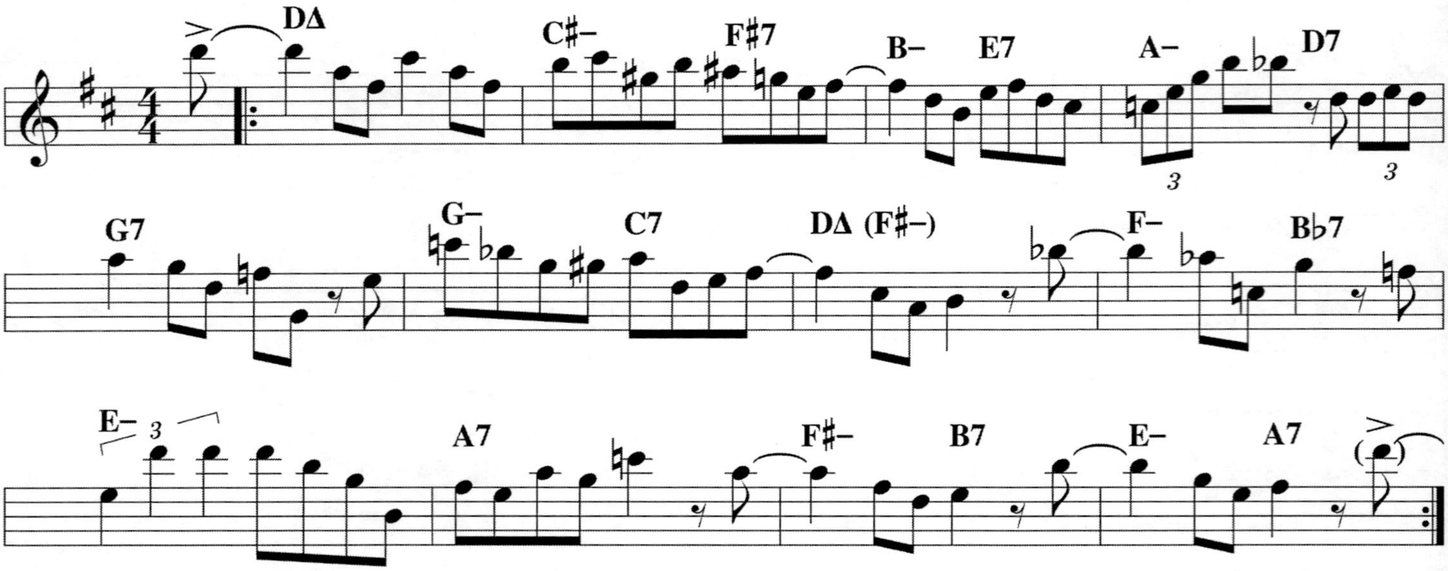
DΔ
C♯– F♯7
B– E7
A– D7
G7
G– C7
DΔ (F♯–)
F– B♭7
E–
A7
F♯– B7
E– A7

SOLOS

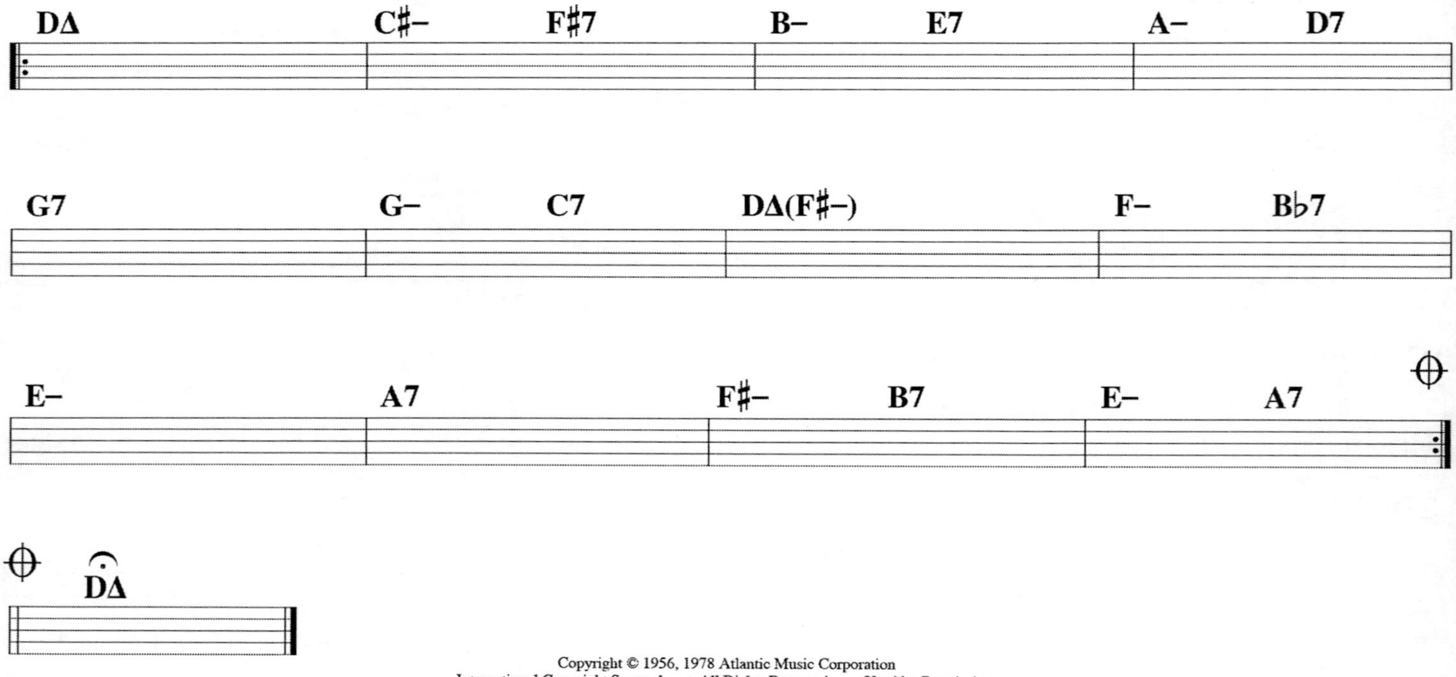
DΔ
C♯– F♯7
B– E7
A– D7
G7
G– C7
DΔ(F♯–)
F– B♭7
E–
A7
F♯– B7
E– A7
DΔ

11. Good Bait

PLAY 3 TIMES (♩ = 108)

By Tadd Dameron & Count Basie

(Lead sheet in Eb with chord changes: GΔ E– A– D7 GΔ E– A– D7 / D– G7 CΔ F7 B– E7b9 A– GΔ D7; BRIDGE: GΔ D– G7 CΔ A– D– G7 C A– / D– G7 CΔ C7 FΔ Bb7 E– A7b9 D– G7b9 CΔ D7)

SOLOS

| GΔ E– | A– D7 | GΔ E– | A– D7 | GΔ G7 | CΔ F7 | B– E7 A– D7 | GΔ D7 | / / / / |

| GΔ E– | A– D7 | GΔ E– | A– D7 | GΔ G7 | CΔ F7 | B– E7 A– D7 | GΔ G7 | / / / / |

BRIDGE

| CΔ A– | D– G7 | CΔ A– | D– G7 | CΔ C7 | FΔ Bb7 | E– A7 D– G7 | CΔ D7 | / / / / |

| GΔ E– | A– D7 | GΔ E– | A– D7 | GΔ G7 | CΔ F7 | B– E7 A– D7 | GΔ D7 | / / / / |

| G | E7b9 | GΔ E7 A– D7 | G | E7+9 | G | E7+9 A– D7 | G | / / / / |

12. Take The 'A' Train

PLAY 4 TIMES (♩ = 112)

By Billy Strayhorn

INTRO
(PIANO CUES-2X)

MELODY

SOLOS

BRIDGE

13. Bye, Bye Blackbird

By Mort Dixon & Ray Henderson

PLAY 6 TIMES (♩ = 138)

SOLOS

Play 4 Times

BREAK

14. Speak Low

E♭ E♭

By Kurt Weill & Ogden Nash

PLAY 3 TIMES (♩ = 116)

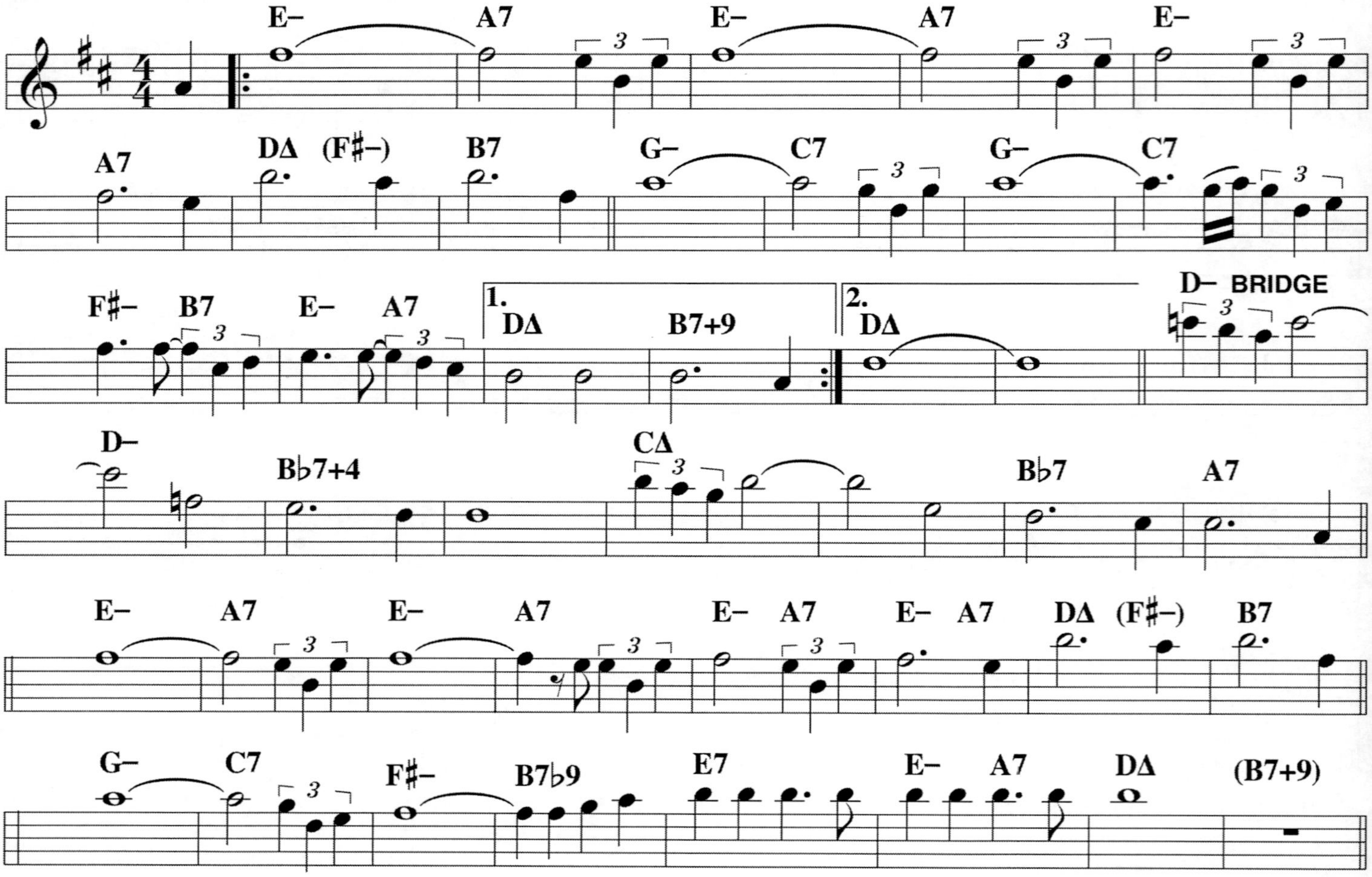

SOLOS

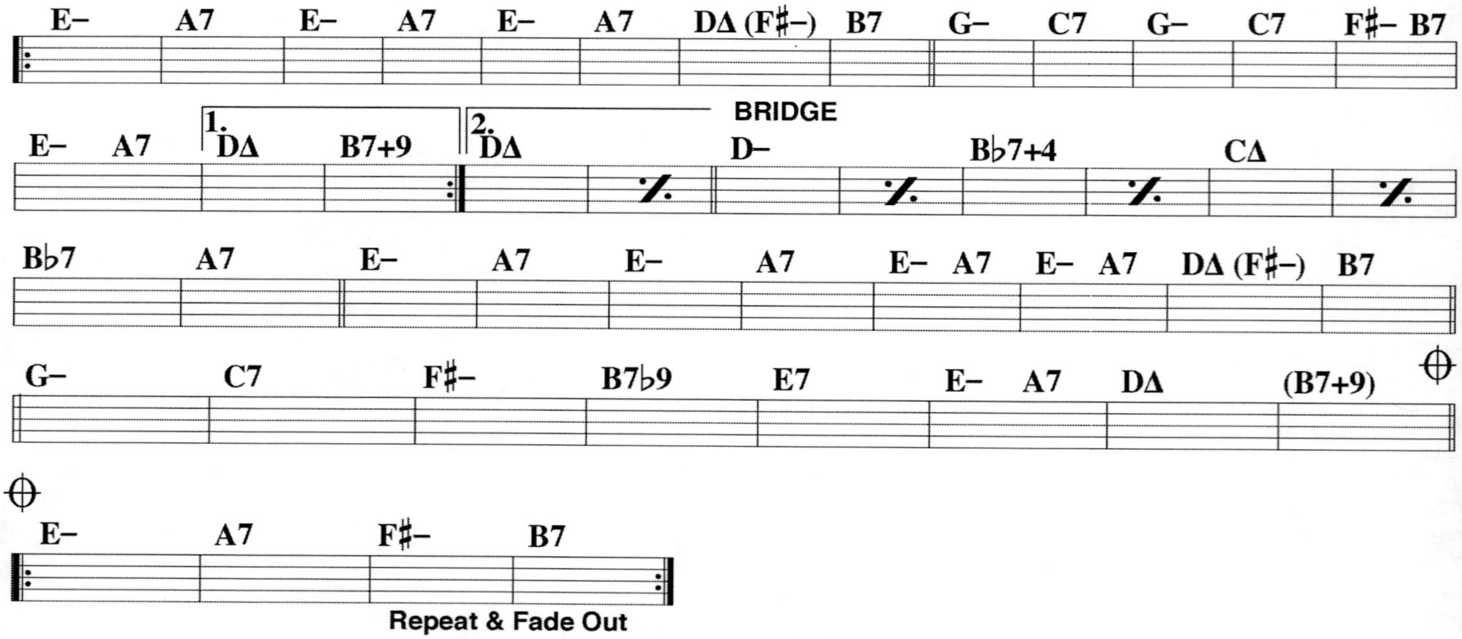

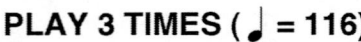

15. But Not For Me

By George Gershwin & Ira Gershwin

PLAY 4 TIMES (♩ = 150)

SOLOS

Repeat Over & Over & Fade Out

Eb

16. Mean To Me

Eb

By Fred E. Ahlert & Roy Turk

PLAY 3 TIMES (♩ = 104)

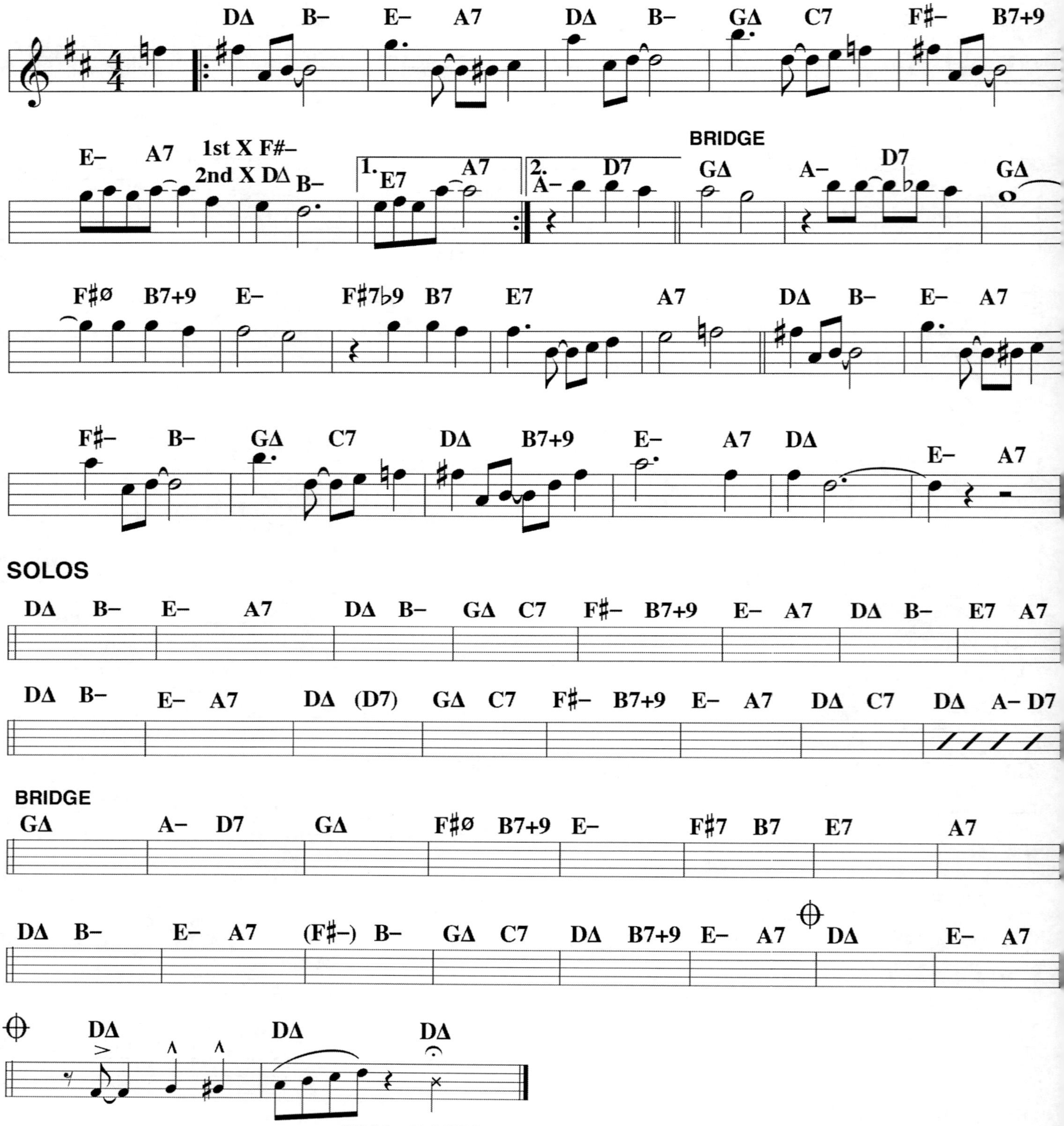
DΔ B– E– A7 DΔ B– GΔ C7 F♯– B7+9
E– A7 1st X F#– 2nd X DΔ B– 1. E7 A7 2. A– D7
BRIDGE
GΔ A– D7 GΔ
F♯ø B7+9 E– F♯7♭9 B7 E7 A7 DΔ B– E– A7
F♯– B– GΔ C7 DΔ B7+9 E– A7 DΔ E– A7
SOLOS
DΔ B– E– A7 DΔ B– GΔ C7 F♯– B7+9 E– A7 DΔ B– E7 A7
DΔ B– E– A7 DΔ (D7) GΔ C7 F♯– B7+9 E– A7 DΔ C7 DΔ A– D7
BRIDGE
GΔ A– D7 GΔ F♯ø B7+9 E– F♯7 B7 E7 A7
DΔ B– E– A7 (F♯–) B– GΔ C7 DΔ B7+9 E– A7 DΔ E– A7
DΔ DΔ DΔ

17. Confirmation

PLAY 5 TIMES (♩ = 116)

By Charlie Parker

SOLOS

BRIDGE

fine = D7+4

18. Oleo

PLAY 8 TIMES (♩ =200)

By Miles Davis

MAY BE PLAYED DOWN ONE OCTAVE

BRIDGE

SOLOS

BRIDGE

19. Moment's Notice

E♭ E♭

PLAY 6 TIMES (♩ = 176)

By John Coltrane

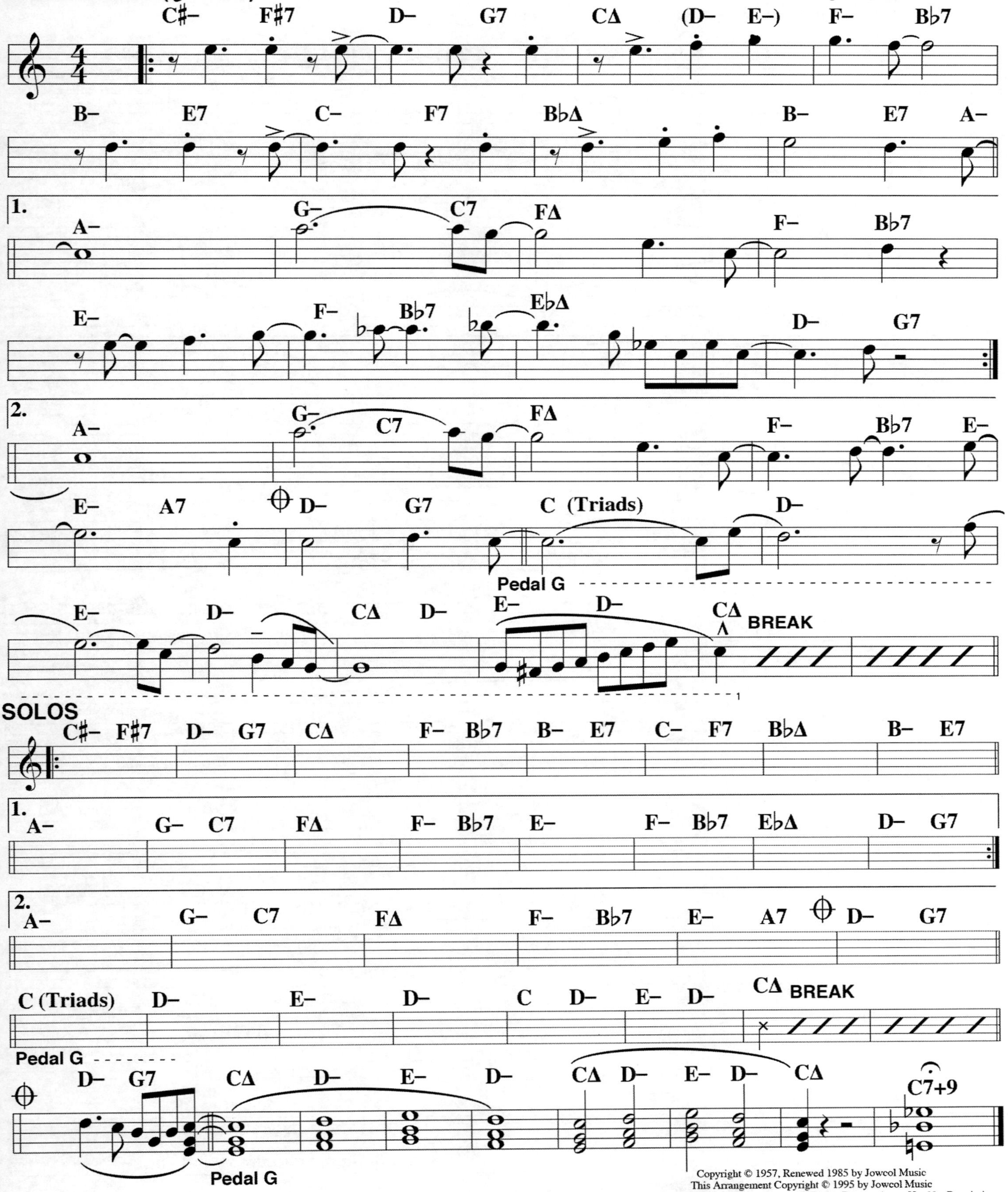

20. Stablemates

(The form in measures = 14–8–14)

By Benny Golson

PLAY 4 TIMES (♩ = 112)

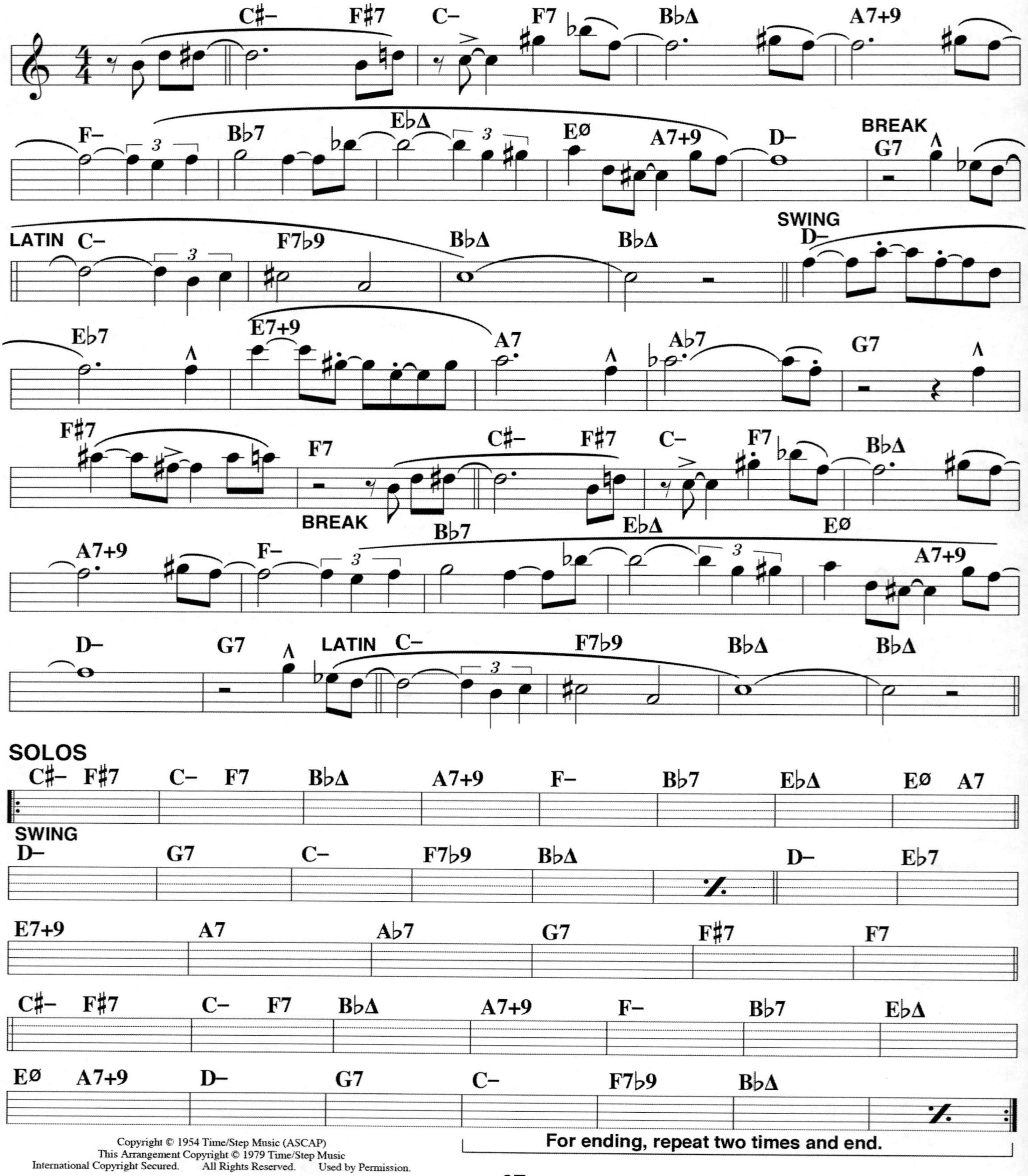

C♯– F♯7 C– F7 B♭Δ A7+9
F– B♭7 E♭Δ EØ A7+9 D– BREAK G7
LATIN C– F7♭9 B♭Δ B♭Δ SWING D–
E♭7 E7+9 A7 A♭7 G7
F♯7 F7 C♯– F♯7 C– F7 B♭Δ
BREAK
A7+9 F– B♭7 E♭Δ EØ A7+9
D– G7 LATIN C– F7♭9 B♭Δ B♭Δ
SOLOS
C♯– F♯7 C– F7 B♭Δ A7+9 F– B♭7 E♭Δ EØ A7
SWING
D– G7 C– F7♭9 B♭Δ D– E♭7
E7+9 A7 A♭7 G7 F♯7 F7
C♯– F♯7 C– F7 B♭Δ A7+9 F– B♭7 E♭Δ
EØ A7+9 D– G7 C– F7♭9 B♭Δ
For ending, repeat two times and end.

21. Algo Bueno

By Dizzy Gillespie

PLAY 4 TIMES (♩ = 142)

The melody has been altered 1/2 step in bars 2 & 6 of the bridge to conform to the altered changes jazz players usually play.

SOLOS

| EØ | A7+9 | DØ | G7+9 | CØ | F7+9 | BbΔ | BbΔ |

BRIDGE

| F− | | F#− | B7 | F− | Bb7 | EbΔ | |

| G− | | Ab− | Db7 | G− | C7 | F7 | |

| EØ | A7+9 | DØ | G7+9 | CØ | F7+9 | ⊕ BbΔ | BbΔ |

| ⊕ BbΔ | C− | BbΔ | C− | BbΔ | C− | BbΔ | BbΔ+4 |

22. Giant Steps

PLAY 11 TIMES (♩ = 110) (Bossa Nova)
PLAY 9 TIMES (♩ = 120) (Swing)

By John Coltrane

NOTE: One recorded version is "Bossa Nova" and the other is "Swing"

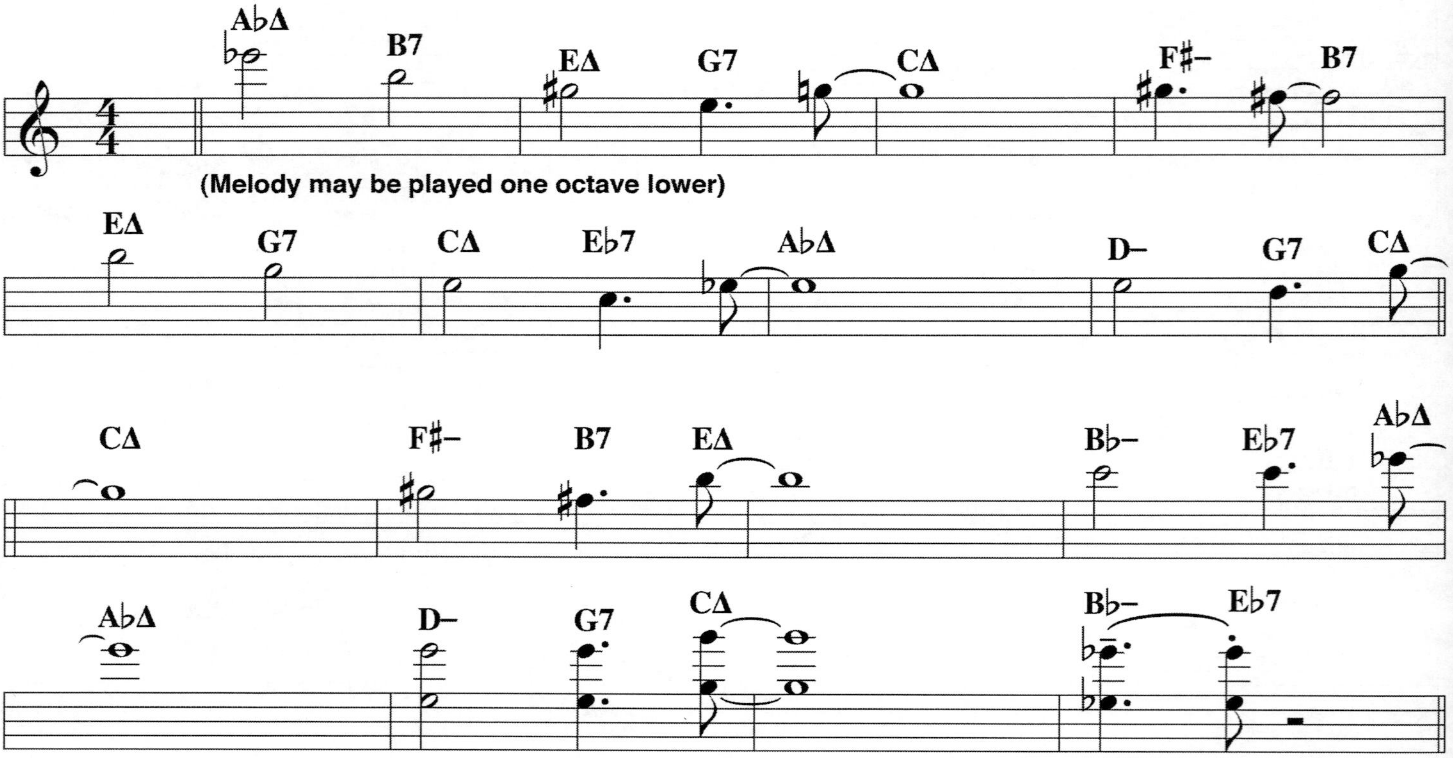

(Melody may be played one octave lower)

SOLOS

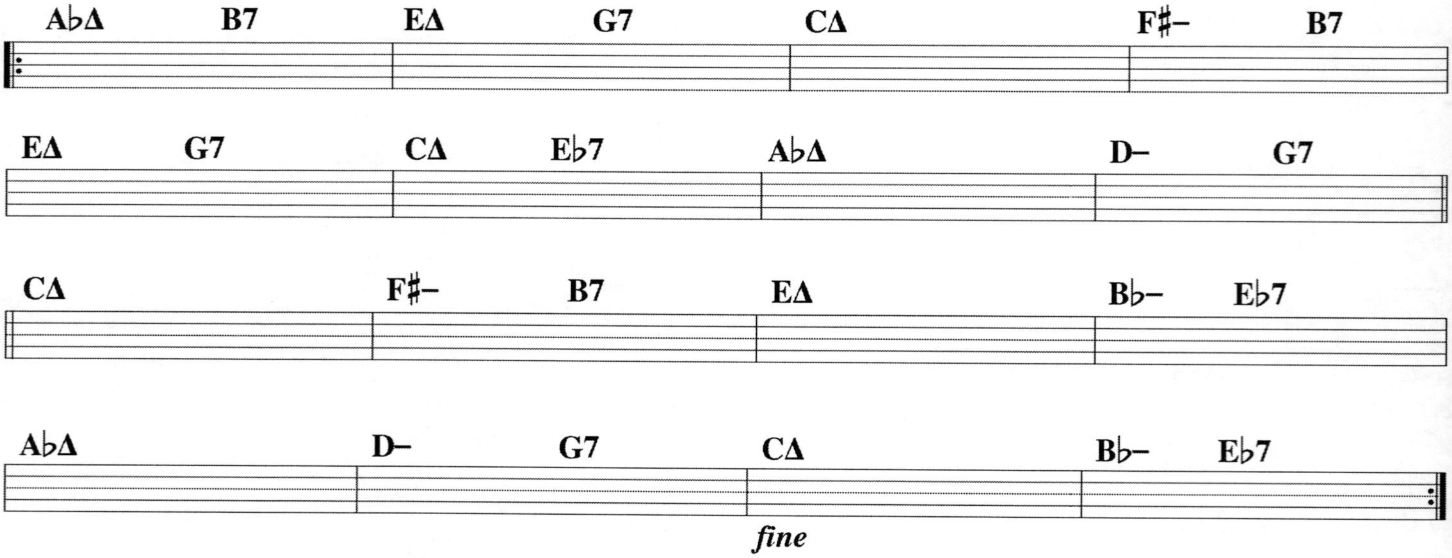

AbΔ	B7	EΔ	G7	CΔ	F#–	B7
EΔ	G7	CΔ	Eb7	AbΔ	D–	G7
CΔ	F#–	B7	EΔ	Bb–	Eb7
AbΔ	D–	G7	CΔ	Bb–	Eb7

fine

1. Four

By Miles Davis

PLAY 5 TIMES (♩ = 132)

(Melody may be played 8va)

BREAK

SOLOS

BREAK

2. Jeannine

3. Tune Up

PLAY 4 TIMES (♩ = 116)

By Miles Davis

SOLOS

BOSSA NOVA

Play 7 Times Then End

4. Perdido

By Juan Tizol

PLAY 5 TIMES (♩ = 132)

SOLOS

BRIDGE

D.C. 2nd Ending

5. Moonlight In Vermont

PLAY 3 TIMES (♩ = 60)   By Karl Suessdorf & John Blackburn

(NOTE: Each Chorus = 28 Measures)

SOLOS

BRIDGE

RITARD LAST CHORUS FOR Eb△ ENDING.

6. September Song

By Kurt Weill & Maxwell Anderson

PLAY 4 TIMES (♩ = 114)

7. Fly Me To The Moon

By Bart Howard

PLAY 6 TIMES (♩ = 140)

SOLOS

PLAY 3 TIMES

BREAK

8. Nica's Dream

By Horace Silver

PLAY 3 TIMES (♩ = 112)

Nica's Dream-Cont.

SOLOS

Bb-Δ		Ab-Δ	
𝄆	./.		./.

Bb-Δ		Ab-	Db7
	./.		

Ab-	Db7	GbΔ (Db7)	C7+9

CØ	F7+9	Bb-Δ	
			./. 𝄇

BRIDGE

Eb-/Ab	Ab7	DbΔ	Bb7b9
𝄆			

Eb7	Eb- Ab7	DbΔ	**1.** E- A7	**2.** F7+9

Bb-Δ		Ab-Δ	
	./.		./.

Bb-Δ		Ab-	Db7
	./.		

Ab-	Db7	GbΔ (Db7)	C7+9

CØ	F7+9	Bb-Δ	⊕
			./.

⊕ Bb-Δ	Ab-Δ	F#-Δ	E-Δ	CØ	F7+9	Bb-Δ
					▬	

BREAK

78

9. Along Came Betty

By Benny Golson

PLAY 4 TIMES (♩ = 116)

SOLOS

fine

10. Blues For Alice

By Charlie Parker

PLAY 10 TIMES (♩ = 108)

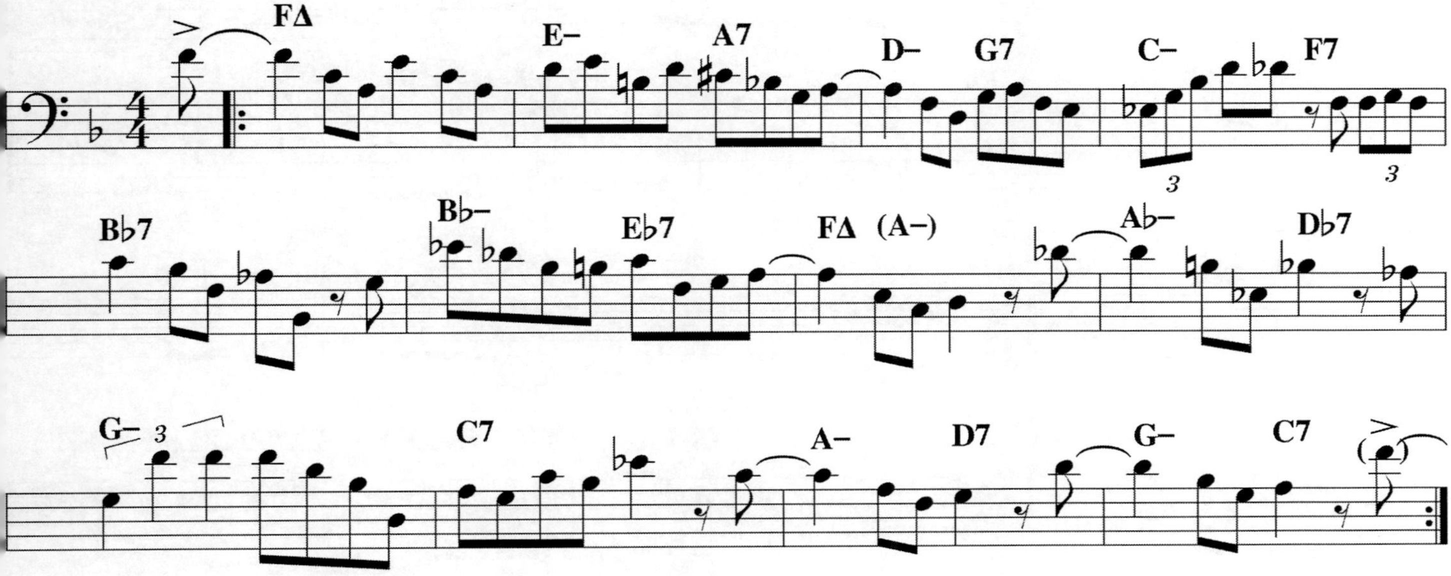

SOLOS

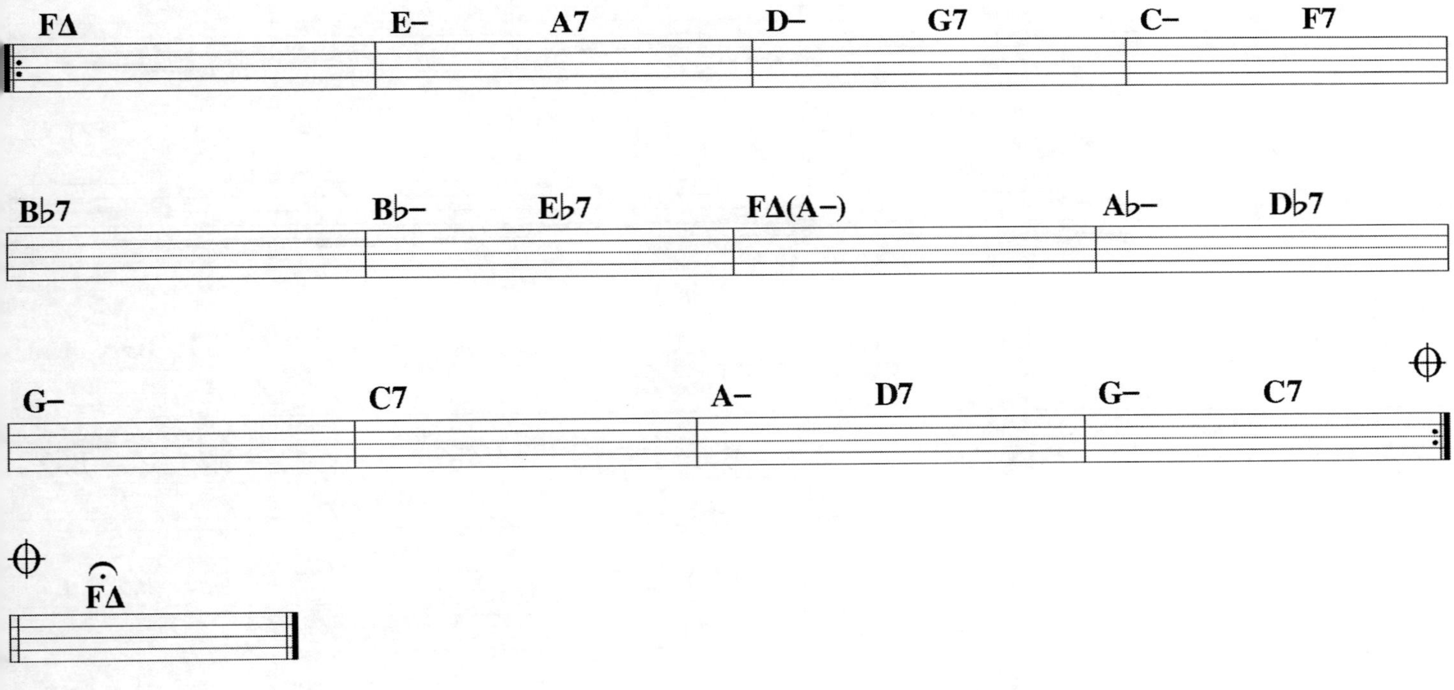

11. Good Bait

PLAY 3 TIMES (♩ = 108)

By Tadd Dameron & Count Basie

12. Take The 'A' Train

PLAY 4 TIMES (♩ = 112)

By Billy Strayhorn

INTRO   (PIANO CUES-2X)

MELODY

BRIDGE

SOLOS

BRIDGE

13. Bye, Bye Blackbird

By Mort Dixon & Ray Henderson

PLAY 6 TIMES (♩ = 138)

14. Speak Low

By Kurt Weill & Ogden Nash

PLAY 3 TIMES (♩ = 116)

SOLOS

BRIDGE

Repeat & Fade Out

15. But Not For Me

By George Gershwin & Ira Gershwin

PLAY 4 TIMES (♩ = 150)

SOLOS

Repeat Over & Over & Fade Out

16. Mean To Me

By Fred E. Ahlert & Roy Turk

PLAY 3 TIMES ($\quarternote$ = 104)

SOLOS

BRIDGE

BRIDGE

17. Confirmation

PLAY 5 TIMES (♩ = 116)

By Charlie Parker

fine = F7+4

18. Oleo

PLAY 8 TIMES (♩ =200)

By Miles Davis

BRIDGE

SOLOS

19. Moment's Notice

20. Stablemates

(The form in measures = 14–8–14)

By Benny Golson

PLAY 4 TIMES (♩ = 112)

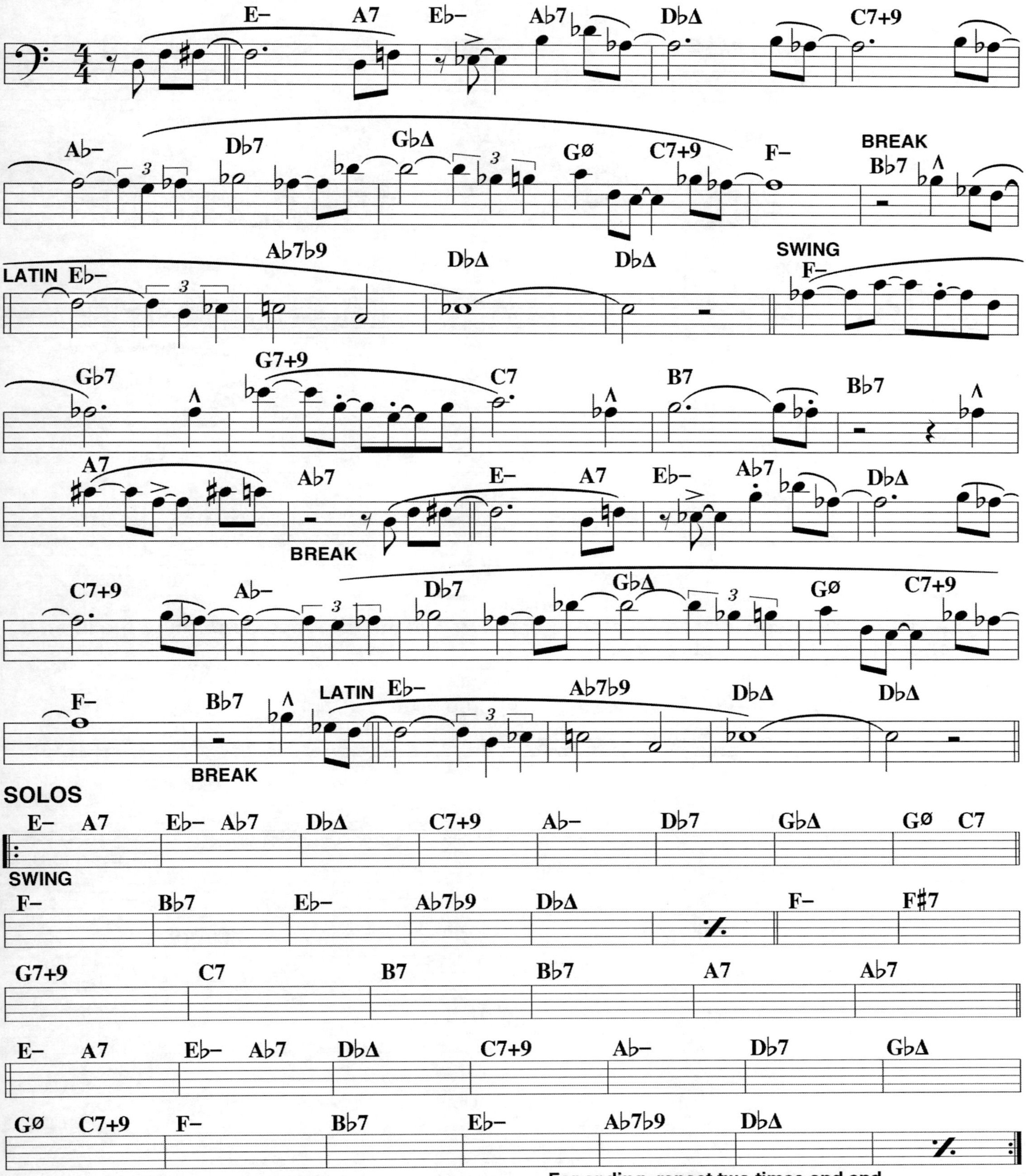
E– A7 Eb– Ab7 DbΔ C7+9
Ab– Db7 GbΔ GØ C7+9 F– BREAK Bb7
LATIN Eb– Ab7b9 DbΔ DbΔ SWING F–
Gb7 G7+9 C7 B7 Bb7
A7 Ab7 E– A7 Eb– Ab7 DbΔ
BREAK
C7+9 Ab– Db7 GbΔ GØ C7+9
F– Bb7 LATIN Eb– Ab7b9 DbΔ DbΔ
BREAK
SOLOS
E– A7 Eb– Ab7 DbΔ C7+9 Ab– Db7 GbΔ GØ C7
SWING
F– Bb7 Eb– Ab7b9 DbΔ F– F#7
G7+9 C7 B7 Bb7 A7 Ab7
E– A7 Eb– Ab7 DbΔ C7+9 Ab– Db7 GbΔ
GØ C7+9 F– Bb7 Eb– Ab7b9 DbΔ

For ending, repeat two times and end.

21. Algo Bueno

By Dizzy Gillespie

PLAY 4 TIMES (♩ = 142)

The melody has been altered 1/2 step in bars 2 & 6 of the bridge to conform to the altered changes jazz players usually play.

SOLOS

22. Giant Steps

PLAY 11 TIMES (♩ = 110) (Bossa Nova)
PLAY 9 TIMES (♩ = 120) (Swing)

By John Coltrane

NOTE: One recorded version is "Bossa Nova" and the other is "Swing"

BΔ D7 GΔ Bb7 EbΔ A– D7

GΔ Bb7 EbΔ F#7 BΔ F– Bb7 EbΔ

EbΔ A– D7 GΔ C#– F#7 BΔ

BΔ F– Bb7 EbΔ C#– F#7

SOLOS

BΔ   D7   GΔ   Bb7   EbΔ   A–   D7

GΔ   Bb7   EbΔ   F#7   BΔ   F–   Bb7

EbΔ   A–   D7   GΔ   C#–   F#7

BΔ   F–   Bb7   EbΔ   C#–   F#7

fine

It's 'Bout Time   #DTRCD-102
One For Daddy • Chicken Pickin' • Emily • It's 'Bout Time! • Sweet Nancy • Amazing Grace • Home At Last • Soul Eyes • I Thought About You • Never Let Me Go • What! Not Another Greasy Spoon?

HANK & FRANK   #DTRCD-034
Kathern The Great • Your Basic Gospel Tune • Basie-cally Speaking • Saving All My Sweet Hugs 4U • Paris In April • Just A Closer Walk With Thee • If I Had You • The Very Thought Of You • Stolen Sweets • Rhythmesque

Groovin' It   #DTRCD-012
Soft Winds • Killer Joe • Jim Dawg • Misty (Ballad) • Easy Talk • Battle Hymn Of The Republic • Just Friends • And What If I Don't • Tenderly • Teach Me Tonight • Misty (Swing)

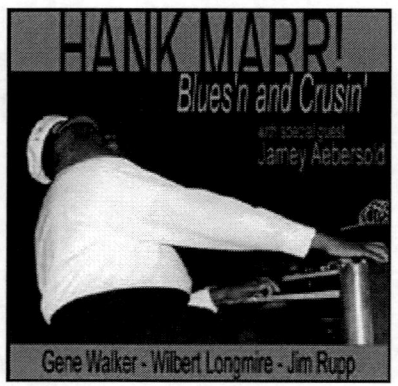

Blues'n And Crusin'   #DTJ1001
A Half-Step Thang • Bluesin' & Crusin • Silver Lining • Blues Thang • A Swingin' Bossa Nova • I'm Glad There Is You • We B 3'in You • Satin Doll • You've Changed • This Little Light Of Mine

HANK MARR

Hear Hank Marr playing his favorite tunes! These recordings are Hank's statement of what an organ recording is supposed to sound like. Great organ groove feels with top rhythm sections and horn players including:

- Jamey Aebersold (Alto Sax)
- Gene Walker (Tenor Sax)
- Frank Foster (Tenor Sax)
- Cal Collins (Guitar)
- Kevin Turner (Guitar)
- Wilbert Longmire (Guitar)
- Jim Rupp (Drums)
- Bill Stewart (Drums)

These groups are tight and "in the pocket" on all the hits and jigs. Check out Hank's version of "Amazing Grace" on "It's 'Bout Time" where he lets it all hang out by doing some talkin' and preachin'!

MEMORIES OF HANK MARR

When jazz education was in its infancy, who could have foretold a time when the oldest, best known, and most highly respected summer workshop would have a world-class jazz organist on its faculty? Taxing credibility even more would have been a prediction that a Big Ten Unive (Ohio State) would have that same person as a member of its world renowned faculty. That man was the brilliant organist and professor of Hank Marr.

One of the most important by-products of the so-called hard bop era was the coming-of-age of the organ in contemporary jazz. The work of important organ pioneers as Fats Waller, Count Basie, "Wild" Bill Davis and Milt Buckner foreshadowed the rise in popularity of various o ensembles, particularly the organ trio, quartet and quintet.

The instrument of choice for the jazz organist was the Hammond B3, which was developed primarily in the gospel church. In 1956, Jimmy Sr more than any other single figure, made the music world aware of its potential as a vehicle capable of playing contemporary jazz; and by end of the decade, virtually every urban area in the US with a sizeable black population and an active jazz scene could boast any number of clubs, and after hours joints that offered an organ group of some sort as nightly or weekend entertainment. Indianapolis, where I grew up, no exception. There were half a dozen local groups including one destined for much greater things, that being the original Wes Montgomery with organist Melvin Rhyne and drummer Sonny Johnson. Visiting groups included famous and soon-to-be-famous groups such as those le Jack McDuff, Jimmy McGriff, Johnny Hammond Smith, Groove Holmes, and the inimitable Hank Marr.

I first heard Hank Marr live in the early 1960s at the Hub Bub, Wes Montgomery's stronghold and one of Indianapolis' most popular bistr was already familiar with Hank's work through some of his early recordings on the Federal label (*Tonk Game, The Push, Mexican Vodka*) an the King label (*Greasy Spoon, Hank's Idea,* The *Marr-ket Place*) which featured the legendary saxophonist Rusty Bryant. As impressive as t recordings were, nothing in them prepared me for one of the most electrifying performances I had ever experienced - a skillful blending o rhythmic aspects of the jump bands of the 1940s (such as those of Tiny Bradshaw, Bill Doggett, and Louis Jordan) and the energy and harm sophistication of the post bebop language. Even the occasional squeak of the organ keys lend authenticity to the golden era of the B3. Ha playing *still* elicits that kind of response from me and from the rest of his many admirers!

From my vantage point as a jazz educator, one of Hank's most important contributions is that of keeping alive the rich and venerable traditic teaching and promoting the organ and the organ combo in jazz. In addition, as his colleague at the Jamey Aebersold Summer Jazz Worksh I have also seen this remarkable man as an inspired and inspiring teacher; a warm, imaginative, sensitive accompanist; a brilliant lecturer, above all, a caring, compassionate human being. **Viva jazz organ! Viva Hank Marr!**

-- David N. Baker, May 1